# The Little Blue Book of Marketing

# The Little Blue Book of Marketing

**BUILD A KILLER PLAN
IN LESS THAN A DAY**

PAUL KURNIT AND STEVE LANCE

PORTFOLIO

PORTFOLIO
Published by the Penguin Group

Penguin Group (USA) Inc., 375 Hudson Street, New York, New York 10014, U.S.A. •
Penguin Group (Canada), 90 Eglinton Avenue East, Suite 700, Toronto, Ontario, Canada
M4P 2Y3 (a division of Pearson Penguin Canada Inc.) • Penguin Books Ltd, 80 Strand,
London WC2R 0RL, England • Penguin Ireland, 25 St. Stephen's Green, Dublin 2, Ireland
(a division of Penguin Books Ltd) • Penguin Books Australia Ltd, 250 Camberwell Road,
Camberwell, Victoria 3124, Australia (a division of Pearson Australia Group Pty Ltd) •
Penguin Books India Pvt Ltd, 11 Community Centre, Panchsheel Park, New Delhi–110 017,
India • Penguin Group (NZ), 67 Apollo Drive, Rosedale, North Shore 0632, New Zealand
(a division of Pearson New Zealand Ltd) • Penguin Books (South Africa) (Pty) Ltd,
24 Sturdee Avenue, Rosebank, Johannesburg 2196, South Africa

Penguin Books Ltd, Registered Offices:
80 Strand, London WC2R 0RL, England

First published in 2009 by Portfolio,
a member of Penguin Group (USA) Inc.

1   3   5   7   9   10   8   6   4   2

LIBRARY OF CONGRESS CATALOGING IN PUBLICATION DATA

Kurnit, Paul
The little blue book of marketing : build a killer plan in less than a day / Paul Kurnit and
Steve Lance.
p.   cm.
ISBN 978-1-59184-305-4
1. Marketing–Handbooks, manuals, etc.   2. Leadership.   I. Lance, Steve.   II. Title.
HF5415.K844   2010
658.8'02—dc22        2009035929

Printed in the United States of America
Set in Minion Pro with Helvetica Neue
Designed by Daniel Lagin

*To Susan, Ara, and Jesse.*
*For fulfilling the best Plan imaginable.*
*—Paul*


*To Carole, Max, and Dan.*
*For everything they've meant to me.*
*—Steve*

# Contents

# Part Two

## TOPICS TO COVER FOR A SUCCESSFUL MARKETING PLAN IN A DAY

### SECTION THREE: WHERE ARE WE NOW?

### SECTION FOUR: WHERE ARE WE GOING?

### SECTION FIVE: HOW WILL WE GET THERE?

## SECTION SIX: CONGRATULATIONS!

## SECTION SEVEN: HIGHWAYS AND BYWAYS

# The Little Blue Book of Marketing

# Introduction

WHERE ARE YOU NOW?

WHERE ARE YOU GOING?

HOW WILL YOU GET THERE?

## WHAT'S YOUR PLAN?

What if you could build a plan that everyone in your organization—from the CEO to the newest hire—agreed on and could embrace . . . *in less than a day*?

What if you could build a plan that had clear objectives, identified your priorities, outlined your budget, and highlighted critical action steps . . . *in less than a day*?

What if you could build a plan that was perfectly customized to your organization's needs and shaped the direction of your company over the next six, twelve, or eighteen months . . . *in less than a day*?

What if you could build a plan that got everyone in your organization on the same page working toward the same objectives . . . *in less than a day*?

What if you could build a plan that put an end to endless meetings, which always lead to more meetings . . . *in less than a day*?

What if you could build a plan that would be an easy-to-follow blueprint and action outline for your company or organization . . . *in less than a day*?

What if you could build a plan that would be fun to do, get input from all your key stakeholders, and bring great ideas to the surface . . . *in less than a day*?

What if you could build a plan customized to your specific needs (e.g., Annual Plan, New Business Start-up, New Product Launch, New Web Initiatives, Raise Money for the PTA, or even Get Your Kid into College—you name it) . . . *in less than a day*?

That's what *The Little Blue Book of Marketing* is all about: building a smart, collaborative marketing plan that your team can develop *in less than a day*. You and your team can put together a Marketing Plan in a Day (MPD) for your company, business, brand, B2B (Business to Business), B2C (Business to Consumer), start-up, not-for-profit, association, organization, club—whatever—in a day. That's seven hours or less (eight hours if you take a leisurely break for lunch).

No mumbo jumbo. No complex, unreadable spreadsheets. Just a simple, clear, concise plan that anyone can understand—and buy into.

And best of all, it's a document you will develop in a single day!

So what's your plan?

"To provide customers with a first-class experience every time they buy our product or service." No, sorry, that's a mission statement.

"To increase sales by 10% over the next 12 months." No, sorry, that's a marketing objective.

"To spend 40% on television, 20% on print, and 20% on the Internet." No, sorry, that's a budget allocation.

How are you going to get from where you are to where you want to be? And while we're on the subject, does everyone in your organization agree on where you are and where you want to be? Got a ready answer to that question?

Competitive pressure, economic upheaval, technological change, global developments (even for mom-and-pop operations), and digital innovation now more than ever underscore the urgent need for a clear, workable marketing plan. Knowing where you're going and how you're going to get there is vital to your company's success. It always was, and it's now more critical than ever.

- You're preparing next year's marketing budget. You need a plan outlining your exact priorities for your agency, media company, and Web team . . .

- You're making key hires at your new job. A candidate asks you if she can read your company's marketing plan. You have her sign an NDA (Non-Disclosure Agreement) , pull a copy out of the file, and hand it over . . .

- The CEO and CMO are reviewing company strategy for the coming year. The CMO is able to bring an up-to-date marketing plan that reflects a realistic assessment of goals, objectives, targets, and action initiatives to get there . . .

- Someone asks you what your company's objectives are and you can rattle off your elevator speech without having to think about it . . . and everyone in your department and the company can give anyone exactly the same pitch . . .

- Your marketing group has to make a presentation to (pick one or all of the following):

✓ the CFO
✓ the CEO
✓ the board of directors
✓ the investors and shareholders
✓ the venture capitalists
✓ the new head of sales
✓ a national trade show
✓ your friends and family who are investing in your business

   You're able to load your marketing plan onto your laptop and head out the door to make the presentation . . .

- Someone in the organization has proposed a new marketing initiative. You're able to review it in the context of your plan to easily decide if the initiative fits your strategy . . .
- Your entire marketing team knows what the overall marketing objective is for your company. They also know who is responsible for what aspect of that objective and how each person's assignment fits in the overall scheme . . .

The Marketing Plan in a Day will get you there—and beyond! It's simple and comprehensive.

It's fully customized to your business or brand needs.

It encompasses all marketing plan elements that will drive business action: Marketing Objective, Strategies, Brand Positioning, Target Audience, Competitive Factors, Budget, Paths to Market, and Action Plan. Whatever you want, whatever you need. And just in case you think those terms are too lofty for your annual bake sale, you'd be amazed how organized and more efficient (shorter) your planning meetings become when you focus your fellow volunteers around all the key issues.

There are plenty of consultants who will come and live in your company for a month (or two or three) and then pontificate about where you need to be. They leave in a cloud of dust without a clear, easy-to-implement plan of how you're going to get there.

Similarly, there are piles of marketing books and textbooks that go on and on about the minutiae of the planning process. Virtually all of them are either impossible to read or opaque to execute.

Neither consultants nor textbooks will get you where you need to be. In both cases, you're relying on outside expertise to show you how to dig out information you already have. The irony is that no one could do it better than you!

Everyone in your marketing department already has one or more pieces of the puzzle in their head. They're executing against it every day. Your researchers likely know all the key research data. Your strategic planners have a good take on your customer. Your directors and managers know the specific assignments they've got to complete (if you even have those various players in your operation). Your CEO, CMO, and CFO all have their agendas (hopefully identical ones). But no one's put the whole puzzle together in one place, in one document, for all to see and for all to manage against. It's analogous to putting together a jigsaw puzzle where each person is assigned a certain number of pieces and a certain section of the board—but possibly not the section where their pieces belong. And NO ONE has a picture of what the completed puzzle is supposed to look like.

So how are you going to do it? You're going to bring everyone who matters into a room. These are your business stakeholders. Participants will show up at 8:00 A.M.—okay, make it 8:30—for coffee and continental breakfast (ooh, aren't we classy?), 9:00 for the actual session, and by 1:00 or 4:00 they'll leave totally exhausted . . . and exhilarated. They will have spent one of the toughest days of their careers doing what they've been paid to do all along—thinking about your product, your service, your brand, your company, your mission, and your goals.

At the same time, they'll leave totally energized. Possibly for the first time in their careers, they'll have a clear understanding of exactly where they want to take your product or service and exactly how to get there. They'll feel immersed in the process and integral to the anticipated results. They'll feel included in a team and empowered to advance the plan.

During your day, as you proceed to develop the plan, your session leader will capture the meeting notes on an easel pad and someone else will enter the notes as slides on a laptop as a first step to building the finished PowerPoint presentation, the Marketing Plan in a Day.

You'll come up with direction and solutions on the spot. You'll pool all the information and knowledge that's in everyone's heads and write it up on the wall so everyone can see it all emerge, evolve, and grow in one comprehensive session. Everyone will be committed. Everyone will reach agreement. Everyone will be ready to take positive action.

Best of all, it will be *your* plan. Not ours, not some consultant's, not some textbook exercise. You won't have to go looking for numbers and research and information you don't have in order to complete a one-size-fits-all template that some marketing professor or strategic guru has created as a theoretical ideal.

That's what *The Little Blue Book of Marketing* is all about. This is a step-by-step user's manual that will show you how ***you can lead the session you need for the situation you're in.*** Your business. Your personalized, customized plan.

Wow.

Yeah, we know . . . we're pretty impressed ourselves! Because every time we facilitate a Marketing Plan in a Day, all kinds of different magic happens. Time and again we're dazzled by what people come up with in these sessions. It's not something we tell them or show them or teach them or make them fill out. It's the stuff they already know that's lying around in their hearts, minds, and files in bits and pieces.

You already have the information.

You already have the expertise.

Applying the Marketing Plan in a Day can transform your marketing approach and business direction. It can be done. We promise. Here are some examples:

- The marketing department of a major corporation realized their same old budget was delivering an ever-smaller media plan and achieving declining results. They needed to address a new integrated marketing model, reallocate budgets, and determine new opportunities. Their MPD helped the entire team refocus their objectives and reallocate a multimillion-dollar budget. The plan was developed in a day.

- A dot-com entrepreneur was pitching his new Web site to investors, sponsors, and consumers with a presentation deck that talked about the bells and whistles of the product but lacked any benefit proposition for consumers (and investors). His advisers and principal backer gathered for an MPD session and developed a new business launch deck, complete with strategy and sales message, in under four hours.

- A national marketing association had a mission and a goal—but no plan of how to achieve them. In four hours they focused their sales objectives, growth strategy, and tactics and developed a new theme to motivate and rally the efforts of their entire marketing and sales staff.
- The sales manager of a small company was spending three days a week on cold calls that produced no leads. Their six-hour MPD identified the company's strengths and weaknesses, clarified their target market opportunity, and set and prioritized their sales message talking points. Sales doubled within four months.
- A nonprofit organization had a lofty vision but no marketing plan. A two-hour session with the founder and the board of directors provided the framework for a comprehensive twelve-, eighteen-, and twenty-four-month plan for getting new funding, driving broader awareness, and engaging pro bono support.

This book will show you how your team can "do it yourself," from developing your customized outline to committing to the time, place, and space for the session to selecting the key players who will address the issues that need to be solved and putting it all in a plan that will strengthen and grow your business.

So take a read. Make your notes. Then bring your company's marketing vision to life. Welcome to the Marketing Plan in a Day. You'll never want to do business without it again.

# How to Use This Book

*The Little Blue Book of Marketing* is organized into two parts:

1. How to Organize and Run a Marketing Plan in a Day
2. Topics to Cover for a Successful Marketing Plan in a Day

Part 1 covers the people, place, props, and planning of the actual session.

Part 2 discusses the marketing issues and variables you will need to address to build your Plan.

Depending on the way you like to organize your thinking, you can read the book in the order we wrote it or you can read part 2 first (the topics) and then go back to read part 1 (the logistics). If you choose to read part 2 first, we suggest you read chapter 6 (Meeting Road Map) first so you understand how the outline for the session can go. Either way, you'll get the knowledge and tools you'll need to successfully plan and run (or run and plan) a Marketing Plan in a Day.

# Part One

## HOW TO ORGANIZE AND RUN A MARKETING PLAN IN A DAY

# SECTION ONE
# COUNTDOWN

GREAT RESULTS ARE ALL IN THE PLANNING. JUST AS THEY teach in the Boy Scouts—"Be prepared"—we've provided a detailed list of what we think is "the right stuff":

- Place and space to hold the meeting
- Facilitator for the meeting
- Planning Partner for the facilitator
- "Guest list" of key stakeholders who will attend and help build the Plan
- Materials you'll need for the meeting

All great recipes combine the best ingredients. These chapters give you the key ingredients to make for a very successful marketing meeting day. Complete these steps well and you'll set the stage for a great Marketing Plan in a Day.

# 1

# Place and Space

"Location, location, location."

—WILLIAM DILLARD

IN REAL ESTATE, THE HIGH-GROUND MANTRA IS "LOCATION, LOCA-tion." The exact same property in a better location—great view, cul de sac, proximity to trains, shopping, etc.—is worth a premium. The same holds true for a Marketing Plan in a Day session. Being in a better location increases the value of your experience as well as the quality of your outcome.

You want a location that's comfortable, accessible, spacious, workable, one that offers no distractions and signals "important." This doesn't mean the meeting needs to be off-site in some fancy hotel or corporate retreat (although a great resort with a spa is always appreciated and might be just what the doctor ordered for your team).

We've seen MPD sessions done at hotels, resorts, and in conference rooms. We've also done them at our offices and those of our clients. They all serve the purpose, but our experience is that the importance of isolating the group from their regular routine and everyday locale—away from their offices and telephones—helps to amp up the energy and focus their thinking.

If you're going to have the session at your own offices, pick a different floor than the one you normally work on. Or pick a conference room that's rarely used. Ultimately, your location decision should be based on four key factors:

## 1. PEOPLE SPACE

Does everyone have room to move around? If there are seven attendees and ten conference chairs, move the three extra chairs out of the room. Give people sight lines to one another. We prefer a rectangular table that's sized for the number of people who will sit around it. Everyone needs space to spread out, to stand up and stretch. To walk around. While some interior designers and industrial architects create "optimal" meeting spaces, we often find that they're filled with oversized conference tables that defeat the intimacy or connectedness of a group meeting room. Make sure everyone's going to be able to get up easily, walk around, and switch places without disrupting the session.

## 2. MEETING SPACE

Is there room for people to meet in smaller groups? Depending on the number of people in your session, during the day you're going to ask people to break into smaller teams and work in groups of three or four in separate corners of the room or separate rooms close by.

Can they do it? Make sure there are areas spacious enough for the breakouts.

Can the space accommodate a separate easel pad and a small group meeting apart from the general space? In a pinch, you can divide up the people around the conference table, but it works better if you can get them into different corners or more isolated spaces.

## 3. EATING SPACE

Where will the group take breaks? Is there a location where you can set up coffee, beverages, and a snack table? Ideally, coffee and water should be available in the room (or just outside it) throughout the day. If your outline leads you to believe you're going to spend more than four hours together, what's the plan and setup for lunch? Lunch can be set up outside in the hallway or even in a very nearby restaurant. When and where you break for lunch should be a conscious decision (built into the outline) regarding whether it will be a working lunch or a real break from the meeting. Either way, there should be an area where people can comfortably chat and meet when taking lunch or other breaks.

## 4. WALL SPACE

This is the most overlooked and most important part of the session. You want plenty of empty wall space. As the session develops, you're going to be writing down the progress of the meeting—the Plan— on large easel pads. Each time you fill a page or cover a topic, number the page (*very important*) and stick it up on the wall so that it can be referred back to at any time. This is the flow of the meeting and the content of the Plan.

Putting all the sheets on the wall is one of the key pieces of magic to the Marketing Plan in a Day. What you're doing is literally creating the Plan presentation in front of the participants' eyes. They can see what they've done, what they're building, and where they're going. They can feel the logic of their thinking and see the outline of their Plan taking shape all around them. They can refer back to earlier pages and reference points that have already been made. We often joke that the meeting is over when the room is covered in easel notes. Turns out it's more often the case than not. There is something very gratifying about seeing and feeling the stuff of the Plan literally surrounding and enveloping the group.

### Marketing Plan in Action

In terms of place and space, we've conducted MPDs in many different locations. Two of the best examples were companies that had the vision to schedule the meeting in their corporate learning centers. Both learning centers were in their buildings, but neither was on the same floor as their offices. Both rooms were spacious, open, customizable in terms of seating . . . and windowless. The four walls were undecorated and readily available for the Plan to be built around the room. There was plenty of room for people to move around. Coffee, water, and soft drinks were on hand in the back of the room at all times. Breakfast morphed into lunch and lunch into snacks, so there was always nourishment—beyond the marketing nourishment—readily available.

There are other great locations you could choose. We keep suggesting the San Pietro Hotel in Positano, Italy. But we digress. . . . Anyway, choose your space wisely, thoughtfully, and effectively. And if you decide you do want to lead your session in Positano, by all means let's discuss how we can help you!

# 2

# Take Me to Your Leader

"Life is like a dogsled team. If you ain't the lead dog,
the scenery never changes."

—LEWIS GRIZZARD

PICK A TEAM LEADER. THE MARKETING PLAN IN A DAY WILL WORK only if there's someone in charge. (Just about everything in life works best if there's someone in charge, but that's the subject of another book.) Ideally, you should pick someone in the middle to senior level of your team who's a rising star and ask that person to be in charge of moderating the session.

We call this person the team Leader. We're also going to call him or her the moderator, session leader, or facilitator. It's all the same thing, but these different labels are expressions of the skill sets the Leader needs to have. This is the person who's going to be preparing the outline, running the meeting, watching the clock, keeping everyone on track, and editing the notes of the day's proceedings.

You can do this yourself with one of your people or you can hire professional facilitators.

But the goal of this book is to make the entire process easy enough for you to do it yourself, empower your people, and power up your organization. As others see how it's done and you see the value of this for all your marketing planning, you can rotate individuals and give them the opportunity to lead future sessions. Making this process turnkey will also encourage you to make the MPD standard practice in your organization.

Ideally, your Leader should be someone who is organized. Someone well liked and respected in your organization. A good listener. Someone who can manage time. Someone who can control what will possibly be (at times) contentious issues and group dynamics. Someone who can keep everyone on purpose. Someone who can take good notes (and has readable penmanship for the easel pads).

On the other hand, you don't want a control freak. The Leader needs to be someone who can keep the session moving ahead productively and smoothly. Someone who can spot opportunities as they arise. It's a tricky balance. That's why we prefer people you see as "management potential" to senior management.

If you're the leader of the business, don't select yourself as Leader. You have too much influence, perspective, subjectivity, and power to be objective or to get honest objective contributions from your other players. People tend to defer to their boss rather than speak their minds. It's human—business—nature. CMOs and department heads tend to be strong-willed individuals who want to move the group in their predetermined direction. They can't help it even with the best of intentions. Keep an open mind about this one: You'll be surprised where the group goes once you've got all the players assembled; and you really don't want to come in with a marketing destination preplanned. You've got a lot to learn in this process, too. Participate, don't manipulate.

### Marketing Plan in Action

In one MPD, the CEO was so concerned that he would dominate the conversation, he suggested he pass on the meeting. He was told that his presence was critically important, but that the Leader would build an outline and a process that would treat him as an equal member of the group, not the organizational head of the company. He was relieved, delighted, and thrilled by the freedom the MPD process gave him as a participant and by the dynamics of the group working together. The camaraderie of the day was a happy by-product that carried forward into follow-up activities as the company went on to execute the Plan.

The CEO felt more integrated with his people and his people felt the CEO to be more accessible.

It takes some important skills to be a good facilitator. We'll mention them here and then you can decide for yourself whether you should be the facilitator or whether someone you know in your organization—or outside your organization—would make a good one.

### 1. ENERGY

Standing in front of the room and coordinating a session for seven hours is hard work. The Leader has to multitask in order to coordinate the room, keep the session moving, think ahead, manage the space, vote, ensure that the outline is covered, and make sure that the end product makes sense, is complete, and that the participants feel a sense of consensus, closure, and productivity. Phew. It's a tall order, and a huge accomplishment for a day. High energy is a must to get through the session. In fact, you might want to think about having two people serve as facilitators. If your session looks to be long and difficult, they can take turns and give each other a break.

## 2. POSITIVE ATTITUDE

People will say all kinds of things at a Marketing Plan in a Day session. At first, some may appear off target, off purpose, or off strategy. You've got to keep an upbeat attitude and give those ideas a chance to be heard. Then figure out where they belong. You'll even have a special easel sheet we explain in chapter 11 (Put Up a Parking Lot) where you can park ideas that come up that are really off topic, outrageous, or fuel for another day. Whether it's in the Parking Lot or the Plan, all ideas that come up should go somewhere on the easel sheets as you move on with the session. Don't squelch anyone's ideas. If you do, those people will start to resist the session and bring down the whole group. Look to refocus them, tease out the worthwhile stuff from the seemingly extraneous or wrongheaded. Enlist others in the room to build on all ideas. Encourage the participant to stay on task in a positive way. And don't worry. We'll be providing you with numerous tools and techniques throughout the book to turn random ideas into big ideas the group embraces.

## 3. EXCITEMENT

Make people eager to attend. You've got to have a good bit of salesperson in you. This isn't anything to dread. In fact, people should be excited to be a part of this, because a lot of issues that keep getting pushed aside in the day-to-day grind of business are going to get their full hearing. (It's our experience that your first Marketing Plan in a Day becomes an effective sales tool for all the next ones. People come away from these sessions energized about the company direction and about their jobs. As they talk about it, they become walking ambassadors for your next session.)

## 4. FLEXIBILITY

The ability to multitask can be a real plus. The Leader has to be a good listener but have a second ear (eye) on the clock and the outline. Are key points being covered? Will there be time to get through the session? Did an idea or roadblock come up that needs to be addressed? You shouldn't be a slave to your outline. If a conversation develops about a key issue, you should be ready, willing, and able to pursue that new direction while deciding which other parts of the outline will need to be streamlined or even dropped. This is a key reason why we believe it's critical that you don't share the outline with the group (other than one other person whom we call the Planning Partner and will talk about in the next chapter). No one else will know that you've strayed from the outline to enable higher-ground conversation. This is also why you might consider having two people run the session. Each can play to his or her strength, and while one is leading the session, the other can be reviewing the timing, the outline, and the schedule.

## 5. A SENSE OF HUMOR

Another real plus in being a great facilitator. A productive Marketing Plan in a Day session is going to get intense. There will be moments when people's private agendas suddenly show up and the naked truth appears. There will be pet peeves and projects people will want to champion. Having a sense of humor can serve to defuse tough situations, ensure progress, keep the session moving, and keep the participants upbeat.

## 6. OBJECTIVITY

If you've read through this entire list and think you have all the qualities listed, then you probably aren't objective and shouldn't be a facilitator. Just kidding (maybe). A good sense of self is always important. But for the MPD, objectivity—or the ability to act objective—is paramount. Which raises the question of whether or not you should use an outside facilitator. If you think there are too many different agendas going on within the organization or you've got your own heavy biases, it might be valuable to bring in an outside facilitator. The person could be from another division, another company, or even be a professional marketing consultant (we'll see you in Positano). If you "go outside," you should choose a facilitator who has all the qualities we've listed here . . . and is acceptable to all the people in the organization.

If you've got all those skills, you've got what it takes. If not, make an assessment of your team and find or train someone who does.

### Marketing Plan in Action

In one MPD training session we assigned four people to practice leading part of the session. One participant was a brand manager who was very headstrong about her points of view. When she got up to lead the session she asked great questions—but then started answering her questions before the group could respond. After we gave her the pointer to engage the group, she elicited single responses from the participants, edited the content on the easel pad to suit her perspective on the issue, and then moved on to her next question (and answer). She, we, and the rest of the training group realized very quickly that she was not cut out to be a good facilitator. She was okay with that. Thank goodness she's a terrific brand manager.

Do you need one person or two? And who should it be? As you're reading this book, think about who would be the ideal person to lead your first session. Pick the person. Give him or her this book to read. Better yet, tell them to buy their own copy. (Our publisher suggested we write that.) Then make sure they understand what they're doing and how they're going to proceed.

In the meantime, read this book yourself so you get a good idea of just what's involved and exactly where you're trying to go.

# 3

# Every Leader Needs a Partner

"Any supervisor worth his salt would rather deal with
people who attempt too much than with those who
try too little."

—LEE IACOCCA

THE LEADER NEEDS SUPPORT. THE LEADER NEEDS SOMEONE TO
bounce ideas off. The Leader needs a collaborator. In other words,
the Leader needs a Planning Partner.

The Planning Partner is the person the Leader is going to work
with in reviewing and optimizing the MPD outline. You're looking
for critical objectivity in the Partner. The Partner needs to be
thoughtful, evenhanded, and constructively critical in the development of the outline and providing good counsel in the planning of
place and people to activate the MPD.

The Planning Partner is the only person with whom the Leader
should share the outline, activities, and exercises ahead of time. This
individual serves to make sure the Leader's outline, process, and
goals are on target. He or she should be someone senior in the organization who's going to be participating in the session.

## Marketing Plan in Action

At an MPD for a national marketing organization, the Leader was the supervisor of training while the CMO gladly accepted the role of participant. This was very empowering for the supervisor, who wanted to look good in front of her boss and ultimately was going to be responsible for implementing the Plan; it was liberating for the CMO, who was integral to the design of the session but could be spontaneous in contributing to Plan development in the MPD session. At another MPD (a major packaged-goods corporation), the division's consumer promotions manager was our Partner, not the brand manager for the product. She was an ideal Planning Partner because she offered a great perspective about the division's best practices without extending specific biases about the brand.

The point we're making is that the Planning Partner should be someone senior who's got a good picture of the overall needs of the organization and can help keep the outline focused. He should be well attuned to the players who will join the session as well as corporate policies, procedures, and pitfalls. The Partner should be a believer in the prospects of the dynamic results an MPD can activate.

The Partner should be a participant, but *only* a participant. The Partner needs to understand that the role of Partner ends when the meeting begins. Once the actual meeting starts, there's only one Leader. As the Leader, don't let the Partner take over the meeting. Set it as a ground rule. Everyone in the meeting is valuable to the process. Everyone has an equal voice.

If you're the head of your department and are itching to be the Leader, take the role of Planning Partner. You'll be able to shape the overall *planning* without taking control of the actual session or Plan.

Once the Marketing Plan in a Day session starts, the person designated as the Leader takes control of the meeting. It's important that the Leader not get sidetracked by secondary issues or people who might grandstand or try to take control of the group. We've got lots of helpful hints throughout the book for how, as the Leader, you can neutralize the would-be hijackers.

# 4

# The Guest List Is Everything

"Hear no evil, speak no evil—and you'll never be
invited to a party."

—OSCAR WILDE

MAKE SURE YOU'VE GOT THE RIGHT PEOPLE IN THE SESSION.
Otherwise you're wasting your time. This idea seems so obvious, but
is actually one of the key concepts of the Marketing Plan in a Day.
Standard operating procedure for most marketing plans is that a
brand manager develops the plan in a vacuum or refurbishes last
year's plan. It's a lonely process and doesn't tap into the best and the
brightest in the organization. Then it goes through an arcane approval process as the ideas are sold in multiple meetings and advanced without the complete commitment of all the people in the
company who matter.

The most important part of the attendance process is that everyone who'll be part of the real-world end-result decision tree is part
of the Marketing Plan in a Day session.

These are the stakeholders! Collaboration is the process of the

THE GUEST LIST IS EVERYTHING

MPD. Consensus is the high ground of the MPD. It can be achieved and activated only if the key decision makers are integral to the development and sign off on the Plan.

Stakeholders come from all centers and circles of your organization. The MPD should be interdisciplinary. Expertise finds its voice from all corners of your organization. Buy-in across disciplines will make marketing action more robust and so much easier to implement. So the "guest list" is critically important. The meeting can handle as many as twelve to fifteen people.

### Marketing Plan in Action

We once ran a session with twenty-two people. There were a lot of stakeholders clamoring to be at the table. The numbers put pressure on everyone having a "voice" on all issues. But we customized the outline to enable issues to be addressed and individual comments and contributions to be recognized. We also broke the group into smaller teams, making sure to mix people from different departments. So you needn't skimp on the invites. A few more bagels might bust your waistline, but they won't bust your budget. And inviting a few more people who have a stake in the outcome of the session and the business will drive a better return on investment every time.

The Planning Partner should play a major role in filling out the guest list. Who will contribute to the Plan? Who has a point of view on the business? Who has a unique perspective on where you are and where you can go with the business? Who are the action players, the team players? Who are the potential impediments, the roadblocks to action? Get them in the session. An MPD session embraces character, creativity, and collegiality. You will learn a lot about your organization and your people in the session. This is an indispensable side benefit of the MPD and will be valuable fuel for future management insights and opportunities.

This is the real world. And in the real world, people who have all kinds of essential or peripheral reasons to be part of the process should be involved:

- If the president of the company is a micromanager who sees and signs off on every business and marketing decision, he should be part of the session.
- If the EVP (executive vice president) of marketing shows all the new campaigns to her husband for his approval, her husband should be part of the session.
- If you have key vendors who are integral to your plans or likely impediments to them (distributors, ad agency, brokers, etc.), include them in the session.
- If the Plan is consumer-centered, identify an insightful, articulate consumer to join the meeting. If you're focusing on a youth-oriented initiative, get a kid or a teen in the room.

We've seen MPD sessions where a varied complement of all those people has been in attendance. It's invigorating. Often for the first time, the team can work with (or confront) an invisible voice that can help enable or scuttle the Plan. Bringing him to the table will be enlightening and efficient by confronting possible Plan pitfalls that the out-of-house customers (trade, consumers, etc.) may react to adversely. That outside person will feel part of the team and can see the impact of what his suggestions have on the group. And, who knows, he may become an invaluable addition to your team for other new initiatives down the road.

Kitchen research is always dangerous. You don't want some stakeholder conveniently restating what his wife or kids feel about a product or initiative. The personal focus group of one or three is never a valuable barometer of consumer opinion. But adding the family member to the MPD can help identify the issues and get at the real truth. Being part of an MPD session makes all participants feel part of the solution. The last thing you want is for your team to spend a day developing the perfect solution only to have someone in the hierarchy—but not in the meeting—kill the whole project because their perspective or goals are different from yours. Ouch! Make sure every guest is a stakeholder and every stakeholder a participant.

We've seen any number of unexpected but inspired choice participants in MPD sessions.

### Marketing Plan in Action

- A major packaged-goods manufacturer included the head of their consumer council (an über-consumer) and the account team from their PR firm.
- A start-up dot-com invited their principal venture capitalist.
- A consumer goods manufacturer that was a family-owned/run business had three brothers, a nephew, and a niece, all in the business, all at the table.
- A foreign-owned manufacturer included the wife of the presi-

dent, who passed judgment on all the advertising and marketing materials produced by the company.

One of the problems you need to actively confront is that you don't always know who the right and complete complement of people is—or you won't be able to get your ideal list to the table on any given MPD day. There are corporate silo issues or scheduling predicaments that sometimes prevent you from having key stakeholders in attendance. We've endured situations where we should have had a key person in the room and didn't—and so will you.

### Marketing Plan in Action

A marketer at an MPD session saw the world through his kids' presumed reactions. He should have had one of his kids in the session to keep him honest and to make progress on a Plan he would sign off on. In another MPD, a senior brand person didn't show up at the last minute but made the "executive decision" that she could participate via telephone. Not a complete disaster, but close. Up close and personal is a requirement for the MPD to work. Active, unfiltered dialogue is key to inspired consensus.

The point is that *anyone* and *everyone* who has a say in the approval process should be part of the meeting. In the room. For the entire session. It's not going to be easy. But for goodness sake, it's only a day or less. People waste far more time in endless meetings that take on the same issues over and over but never seem to result in any positive action. People may not readily see the importance or value of what you're doing with the MPD until they're engaged in it and after it's done. So a great invitation—e-mail, in person, memo—matters. Anticipate. If you know you can't get a key stakeholder to the table, invite a "stand-in," her number two in the department or a kid from the senior marketer's school if sonny boy is not available or the marketer doesn't want his kid—or his parenting—exposed to the group.

Explain the MPD in advance to all participants without giving away the specific agenda of the day. Empower everyone to believe that this will really make a great business difference, give them an important seat at the table, and be lots of fun.

Make sure the location, date, and time are convenient for all participants. You want calendars cleared and everyone to be on-site, on time, ready to go. That means no one calling in on a conference call or videoconferencing. This is important in-person stuff. A disembodied voice on the phone or a digitally pixilated person on a monitor doesn't bode well for the group. Distance or a digital divide is, at best, awkward and usually interruptive, counterproductive, or even derailing of the entire process and product of what you're trying to achieve. The results of your efforts will be far more rewarding and actionable if everyone's in it together, gathered together. Kumbaya!

Other problems can include the drop-in manager who shows up at the beginning of the meeting and then exits. Discourage this! A senior player who shows up well into the process to check up on things is a buzz kill. That person establishes himself as superior to and outside of the process. You've got to be a diplomat and salesperson to get all the right people to commit. You've also got to be a realist about the structure of your business. Tact is helpful. Emphasizing the importance of participation to the progress of the business is the winning ticket. Get active buy-in from the most senior people and use them as ambassadors to get the attendance you need.

Finally, don't be afraid to be adventurous to get the participation you know you need. Thinking outside the confines of your organizational chart can pay big dividends.

# 5

# Tools of the Trade

"Dull tools yield dull results."

—PAUL KURNIT

YOU NEED THE RIGHT TOOLS TO GET THE JOB DONE WELL. PENS, paper, easels, food, drink, and work space are all tools. The most important tool is the space—geographic and people space—which we've already covered. Beyond that, there are a number of simple but indispensable tools for your session that you should have on hand long before the session starts.

The following list is what you'll need for a small session of six people or less. For more than six people, you're going to need multiples of these tools to accommodate breakout and other exercise work sessions.

## 1. SESSION OUTLINE

This is your number one tool. Make sure you bring a printout of it as well as your own laptop when you come to the session. This is the moderator guide. It will inform and direct the session, ensuring you get the content you need in the time you've allotted. Bring only two copies of the outline to the meeting: one for you and the other for your Planning Partner. You don't want the participants to know what's coming—you're the guide on this trip.

## 2. LARGE EASEL PADS AND AN EASEL STAND

You'll need one for every four or five people in the room. Throughout the day you're likely going to have breakout exercises and will divide the group into teams of four or five. Each group will need its

own area to work in (that's the space tool to be discussed), and you'll need an easel, easel pad, and markers for each group. If you've got twelve attendees, figure two to three easels, easel pads, and sets of markers. In addition, you'll need two full pads of easel paper for the Leader. You're going to fill anywhere from ten to forty pages with notes as you go. You don't want to run out.

You're going to be sticking the easel pad sheets to the wall, so we recommend Post-it easel pads. (We stuck that in so that maybe someone at 3M will read this and send us a lifetime supply.) Yes, they're expensive (oh, well, so much for the free lifetime supply). Other sticky-backed generic poster pads will work just fine, and they're worth the extra money for their convenience. You don't want to deal with adhesive tape and waste time or energy sticking sheets to the wall. Plus, you can easily move adhesive pages around on the walls if the information flow changes.

## 3. MARKERS

Lots of colors—and lots of backups—are critical for highlighting, underscoring, voting, providing subcomments, adding parenthetical expressions, and tallying votes. One set for the Leader, and an additional set for each additional easel (for subgroup exercises). They should be thick-tipped for bold, visible writing. The Leader can decide which colors drive which content or highlights throughout the day—whatever works best to make the flow of the Plan clearest for all to see and feel as it develops.

## 4. ONE LAPTOP WITH POWERPOINT AND SOMEONE WHO IS A FAST AND ACCURATE TYPIST

This is an important job and should be entrusted to a member of your group who is methodical and accurate. You can select a junior or administrative player if you are comfortable knowing that they may be exposed to pretty weighty—and perhaps controversial—business content. If you appoint him to this "scribe" role, make sure he sees it as a privilege and a learning opportunity to be in the room. Make sure he can take accurate notes and quickly type into PowerPoint everything that's written down on the main easel pad—exactly as it's written. And make sure he isn't someone who wants to get creative with the session. His role is primarily meeting recorder, not meeting participant.

## 5. INDEX CARDS AND/OR STICKY NOTES

Have plenty of these—different colors are also helpful. More is always better because people like to have different material to write on. It makes them and the meeting feel more important. Throughout the meeting, your participants will be writing down their personal answers to questions on the cards or sticky notes. This will enable personalized, unfiltered content to be captured before any group influencing begins. Before the session starts, make sure everyone has at least fifteen to twenty note cards at their seat.

## 6. PENS, PENCILS, AND PADS

Have these on hand so people can take notes. Not everyone will necessarily come equipped with these basics. Having them in place when everyone walks in makes the table—and the meeting—look ready for action. If your business has logoed stationery or writing instruments, use them. After all, this session is all about the brand.

## 7. SMALL, STICKY DOTS OR STARS

This is the actual size of the ¼-inch-diameter dots or stars that come in packs of about five hundred or one thousand in various colors and are usually in the same section of the stationery store as the Post-it notes and the index cards. You'll need these for certain voting activities throughout the day.

## 8. NAME TENT CARDS

Put a name tent card in front of each seat (with the name facing into the room). It's a good way to set seating assignments and mix people up. Don't assume everyone knows everyone else in attendance. And even if they do, it's a nice touch. It sets the MPD meeting apart from everyday meetings. You also might consider moving people's seats around during the session. At the breaks you can rearrange the name cards while they're out of the room.

## 9. TOYS

Literally. Things like Play-Doh. Pipe cleaners. Wind-up toys. Stress balls. Balloons. Magic slates. Nerf swords (in case things need to be settled by a duel). Transformers. K'NEX. Tinkertoys. Ideally, toys that invite open-ended hands-on play, toys that require inventiveness and inspire imagination. This is "hand candy." Just having these toys on the conference table indicates an invitation to play throughout the day: It signals that the session is supposed to be fun (even though it's really hard work). It suggests that the process is a creative one.

## 10. FOOD (AND DRINK)

An absolutely critical tool of the session. As Napoleon so aptly observed, *"C'est la soupe qui fait le soldat"* (loosely translated as "an army marches on its stomach"). The food sets the tone for the entire day. Don't skimp. Especially on the breakfast. Make sure there are plenty of carbs on hand. Juice. Fresh, hot coffee. And keep the coffee, soda, and water readily available throughout the day.

Plan on a great lunch buffet and snacks in the afternoon. Be like your mother and order twice as much as you think you'll need. (Oh, your mother didn't? Hmm. What other issues do you have?) Your mother knew from experience that it's always better to have too much than too little. Keep it coming and make arrangements for new food and beverage deliveries throughout the day. If you're going a full day, candy is always appreciated at about 3:00 P.M., when energy ebbs during the afternoon blood-sugar drain. Remember, "Snickers satisfies you."

When we run MPD sessions in our office, we always provide a good breakfast. The food is one of the first impressions of the day. It should be inviting and satisfying. If we're not catering lunch, we e-mail the participants in advance for lunch orders or take the orders as soon as the participants arrive. We make arrangements with our office manager to call in the order about an hour (or more) before the planned break so that it will arrive fresh and ready just before the break. (Are we sounding a little too focused on food? Maybe it's *our* issues we need to discuss.) Manage your food and beverages well and you'll go a long way toward making the session that much more nourishing, too!

## Marketing Plan in Action

At one MPD the company was really pressed for time and chose to have the session on a Monday morning (not a great idea). There was no coffee or food, people showed up late, and there were no tent cards set out. Everyone in the room knew one another but the outside facilitator didn't know anyone. We quickly made up tent cards for everyone to write their name on to enable the facilitator to be more personal in the session. We gathered lunch orders and began with an icebreaker exercise about weekend highlights to get everyone's head off the weekend and into the business task at hand.

### *Tools of the Trade*

✓ Session outline
✓ Easel pads
✓ Easel stand(s)
✓ Markers
✓ Laptop with PowerPoint
✓ Index cards (and/or Post-it notes)
✓ Pens, pencils, and pads (by each person's seat)
✓ Stickers (dots or stars)
✓ Tent cards
✓ Toys
✓ Food

Have them all on hand and ready to go. Now let's get ready to go ourselves!

## SECTION TWO
# KEYS TO THE KINGDOM

NOW THAT YOU'VE GOT A LIST OF THE PHYSICAL TOOLS, you're going to need the process tools to keep your session moving to accomplish your goals in a day.

This section starts with the Road Map—the outline for the session. Next comes Thought Starters—questions you send participants in advance to prime their thinking for a productive meeting.

Warm-ups and Workouts are exercises that energize your meeting by inspiring content and advancing strategic ideas.

Power Words help focus group consensus around strategic language that will drive your Plan forward. Voting breaks logjams and reveals areas of agreement. The Parking Lot is a vehicle (pun intended) for good ideas not essential to the task at hand but worthy of being captured for future consideration. Finally, we'll give you an overview of how to put all the keys together to best run the actual session.

# 6

# Meeting Road Map

"The will to win is nothing like the will to prepare."

—JUMA IKANGAA, NEW YORK CITY
MARATHON WINNER

NO MATTER WHAT YOU WANT TO ACCOMPLISH OR HOW LONG you've got to achieve it, you're going to need a Marketing Plan in a Day session **outline.** More than an agenda, it's an in-depth road map that ensures you cover all the key issues to meet your Marketing Plan objective. It's as easy as 1, 2, 3:

1. Where Are We Now?
2. Where Are We Going?
3. How Will We Get There?

Simple, right? Great! Glad you enjoyed reading the book—we wish you continuing success in the coming weeks and months.

You want more? Phew, you're a tough audience. But here's our dilemma: If we give you a really detailed outline, you'll follow it slavishly and it won't ever be customized or responsive to your specific needs. On the other hand, if we don't give you detailed counsel on outline building, you'll run the risk of building a meeting that won't fully develop and resolve the issues you're facing in the time you've allotted. That's the elegance of the Marketing Plan in a Day. How YOU design your meeting guarantees that you'll resolve key issues based on robust consensus.

So here's our compromise: The rest of this book will explore these three questions in depth, offering suggestions on how you can draw out the best thinking from your key participant stakeholders in the room. As you read the book, make margin notes or add your notes to chapter 36 (Sample Outlines) about what points resonate with you and are the most important issues for your group to cover. But answering our overarching three questions—in whatever time frame you commit to and whatever priority needs you have—will always be the building blocks for your MPD outline.

Depending on how much time you have and the needs to be addressed, emphasis on each of the three questions will vary. As you integrate the MPD method into your ongoing business process you'll design additional sessions to dust up, brush up, or even overhaul elements of your marketing program that will enrich your business procedures, employee efficiency, and ensure marketing success.

At this point you might want to even scribble down the four or five major needs you most want to address in a marketing planning session with your key business stakeholders. You'll find they'll likely be "center stage" in the ultimate outline you'll design and follow as the guide for your meeting. What will you write? Maybe something like this (if the following outline points seem blind right now, they are. Don't panic. We'll be covering each of them throughout the book):

### 1. Where Are We Now?

- **a.** Business Objective
- **b.** Brand Positioning
- **c.** Competition and Competitive Framework

### 2. Where Are We Going?

- **a.** SWOT (strengths, weaknesses, opportunities, and threats)
- **b.** Opportunity
- **c.** Product Line and Manufacturing
- **d.** Brand Capabilities and Brand Limits

### 3. How Will We Get There?

- **a.** The Big Idea
- **b.** Paths to Market
- **c.** Budget Parameters
- **d.** Marketing Toolbox
- **e.** Action Team and Partners
- **f.** Key Milestones and Next Steps

Right away, you're going to get a good handle on your current situation and a Plan build-out. But maybe you believe you have a good handle on Where Are We Now? and Where Are We Going? Then your outline and your day should put much more focus on How Will We Get There? Your outline might look more like this:

- **1.** Where Are We Now?
  - **a.** Business Objective
  - **b.** Competition

2. Where Are We Going?
   a. SWOT
3. How Will We Get There?
   a. The Big Idea
   b. Paths to Market
      i. Who's Our Market?
      ii. Who's Our Trade?
   c. Marketing Toolbox
   d. The Team
      i. Dream Team
      ii. Action Team
      iii. Partners and Strategic Alliances
   e. Budgets
      i. Budgeting Methods (Bid It, Brand Available, Share of Category, Task)
      ii. Budget Allocation
4. What Does Victory Look Like?
   a. Responsibilities and Timing
      i. Milestones
      ii. Action Timetable
      iii. Who's Responsible?

What outline will be most productive for your business and your participants? Your outline should be your guide, not your taskmaster. It should cover everything you need in your Plan. It should include timing for each section as a test of reasonableness for what you need to accomplish in the meeting time you've allotted (as a general rule, Paul likes to estimate an average of thirty minutes for each major point—some will be fifteen, some will be forty-five—

plus fifteen-minute breaks and a half-hour break for lunch). Remember, it's an intensive session and momentum is important.

Preparing the outline is a creative endeavor, one that's totally customized for every session you do. It's up to you to decide which goal to emphasize in the meeting. That's the power of a good road map. It's also the advantage of not reviewing the outline in advance with anyone but the Planning Partner. It enables and ensures meeting dynamism. The Leader can be nimble in pursuing and drilling into hot topics as they emerge as well as being flexible enough to move outline elements around, possibly eliminating some, in the pursuit of landing on the key issues that matter most.

### Marketing Plan in Action

At one MPD the goal was to set a positioning and future direction for the company, but it became clear early in the planned session that the three principals weren't on the same page in terms of projected growth and future goals. While the initial outline was heavy on "How Will We Get There?" the facilitator had to expand the discussion of "Where Are We Now?" while the MPD was going on. Extending the discussion of the foundation of the company made establishing consensus around future direction much more satisfying for all the players.

By all means, keep your outline handy. Use it as a guide for content and to track timing and objectives. But don't let it tie you down to the point where you miss a valuable insight or disallow an important line of conversation. These issues can be covered in greater detail in the meeting if they advance critical issues on the outline. Or they can be captured in the Parking Lot (chapter 11) for further discussion outside the MPD.

A simple but perhaps counterintuitive tip: Always develop your outline from scratch. Don't cut and paste from work you've previously done. Or work someone else has done. It may seem to be a smart and easy shortcut to get a good outline. It isn't. In fact, it will take you longer to edit from an existing document and you'll come up with a worse outline. Developing a working, viable Marketing Plan process is your opportunity to step back and start with a blank page. Too often a department or company has been running on automatic pilot. You're doing things the way you've always done them. Don't. Start fresh, think fresh, and let the outline pop into your head based on the intuitive items and issues you know the MPD needs to answer. Build a first draft. Then walk away from it. Come back to it hours or even a day later and have at a good edit.

As part of the outline, be sure to build in meeting breaks. Breaks can be strategic. Following a core piece of content, let people take a breath (and a bathroom break). But also be flexible about where and when you will take breaks throughout the day. Be aware of the energy in the room as well as camaraderie as the Plan unfolds. If you are on a roll at 11:00 A.M., even if you had planned a break for that time, don't disrupt the flow by forcing one. And if you're struggling with a particular idea and the group looks fatigued, let everyone get up and get the blood flowing again. Change the energy in the room even if you hadn't planned to break for, say, another thirty minutes.

Start thinking about your outline right now. Put down some questions you feel your team has to answer. Don't worry now about where they will go in your MPD session. Just jot down ideas you want to cover . . . and let's move on. When we've covered all the important session issues you need to know about and plan for, we'll come back to building the road map in-depth in chapter 36 (Sample Outlines). It's a dynamic and critically important process.

# 7

# Thought Starters

"Lead your mind, like a child, gently back to the work
at hand."

—OLD SUFI SAYING

WE ALL NEED A LITTLE SOMETHING TO GET OUR BRAINS GOING
or keep them on track. Especially in a half-day or daylong session
that's going to require every ounce of brainpower and creative thinking your team has.

Oh, did we mention that? Even if we did, let's mention it again: A
Marketing Plan in a Day session might well be the most difficult
(and valuable) exercise your team has ever done. Everyone's going to
have to have their marketing caps on and be willing to bring their A
Game. It's a right-brain-meets-left-brain enterprise—creative, collaborative thinking to land on logical, dynamic planning.

One way to prep and pump up the team is to tease them by
sending out an e-mail in advance of the meeting containing Thought
Starters you want participants to think about. Some examples:

1. What's the most successful new product or service introduced in the last five years—and why?
2. What's the most indispensable technological device in your life—and why?
3. If you couldn't watch television for a week, what would you do with the free time?
4. What's the most successful advertising campaign you can think of? What makes it so great?
5. What was the biggest innovation in your product category in the past five years? What made it successful?
6. If you could have any job in your organization, what would it be—and why?
7. If you could recommend one change in your company to make business better, what would it be—and why?

Thought Starters get your group in a good mind-set for the meeting. They can be closely related to issues you plan or they can be out-of-the-box questions that are fun to cogitate. They may find their way into the actual meeting or simply end up as advance stimulus that enables more efficient group focus in the meeting.

Thought Starters are "blind" in the sense that they're not necessarily focused on the specific business tasks you'll confront in the MPD. That's the idea. You shouldn't tip your hand as to the actual questions you're going to ask in the session; you want to get people's minds working in the general areas you're going to explore. You want your attendees to come to the meeting open-minded and ready to confront issues without the bias of predetermined answers or marketing solutions. The Thought Starters are great fuel for your session—and always available to advance the conversation—but they won't necessarily drive the progress and content of it.

As you develop your session outline, think about different types of Thought Starters you can use as "brain jolts." Simple ways to get people thinking in a different way than they're used to and great inspiration to both prepare them and motivate them for the actual session.

### Marketing Plan in Action

At one MPD with an inventor, the focus was on an inspirational character-based concept. He had a very specific idea of what he wanted to achieve with the business. The Thought Starter questions focused on character design ("Who are other characters you admire most and why?"), content ("What other inspirational messaging concepts resonate with you?"), and paths to market ("What character-based brand has done the most innovative job of marketing in the past three years?"). The result was a much more open discussion among all participants about optimal ways forward for the brand.

You should prepare from five to seven questions and they should be relatively easy to consider and answer. These are questions for consideration, not detailed cogitation or formal written responses. When you feel you're ready to go, brief the attendees (via e-mail) in general terms on what to expect in the meeting, send them the Thought Starters—and remember, don't include the outline!

# 8

# Warm-ups and Workouts

"Opinion is the lowest form of human
communication."

—CAROLE SCHWEID

EVERYONE'S GOING TO SHOW UP TO THE SESSION WITH A PERSONAL agenda, an opinion, and a point of view. Rather than argue with any of that, as the facilitator, the best thing to do is to loosen up their mind-sets. Throughout the day, you'll want to use a series of exercises that will stimulate creativity with outside- (and inside-) the-box thinking to get everyone interacting in a comfortable and inclusive group dynamic. They help keep interest up, consensus in reach, and you moving toward your goals. They come in two forms— **Warm-ups** and **Workouts**—and we've indicated throughout the book which exercises are which.

## WARM-UPS

Warm-ups get the creative juices flowing. They're fun, always interesting, and meant to stimulate thinking. They're relevant to the task at hand, yet removed enough so there's no right or wrong response. They loosen up the group—much as an icebreaker does. They help people get to know one another and extend meaningful input to the strategic questions that need to be confronted. For example:

1. What's the best life decision you ever made?
2. Who's your favorite superhero—and why?
3. What are your favorite movies (or books)?
4. Who was your best boss ever—and why?
5. What's your most indispensable brand?
6. If you were stranded on a desert island, what three music albums would you bring with you?

Some Warm-ups can be really "out there," while others can be closer to your task at hand. But none of them are specific to an issue you need to resolve for your Plan. Besides these, throughout the book you'll read examples of other Warm-ups. We've also included a number of examples in chapter 38 (Sample Warm-ups and Workouts). But we urge you to think of your own for each MPD that you run. Build in time and a place for these in your outline or keep a list handy to best adapt to circumstances in your session. The better you know your own team, the group dynamic, and the objective of the session, the better value you'll realize as you fine-tune our suggestions—and invent your own Warm-ups and Workouts—to fit your specific process and planning goals.

### Marketing Plan in Action

During a two-day session at a conference center, each member of the team was asked to write down his or her three indispensable

Web sites (excluding the five most popular in the United States). A seemingly off-purpose but entertaining sidebar discussion ensued as everyone wanted to know more information about other people's favorites. Hometown preferences were revealed when one participant listed www.redsoxnation.com. Others learned about movies when another participant mentioned www.imdb.com. In all, the exercise revealed new information about each participant, about the personal nature of the Web, and about how people access information. The Warm-up proved tremendously useful to the task at hand, which was about creating a new sticky Web-delivered idea for the brand.

4

## FAVORITE WEB SITES

Yahoo

ESPN

IMDB

Metacritic

HGTV

FoodTV

YouTube

Twitter

Redsoxnation

Kayak

It's been our experience that Warm-ups work best at the start of the session and after breaks. As you get deeper into the session, you'll find more use for Workouts.

## WORKOUTS

Workouts are designed to move Plan content forward. They're integral to the entire day's planning work. You may be better off adopting—or adapting—some of the specific ones we list at the point where we recommend them. But here, too, you'll want to think of customized Workouts to get close to your outline content. We'll give you some examples, but they won't mean as much out of context as they will later on in the book:

- What is the most impressive characteristic of a competitor you admire that you could apply to your brand?
- List the three best line extensions for your brand.
- Develop the worst product idea you can imagine for your company. Then flip it 180 degrees to make it a great idea. (This Workout can best be done as a group walk-around exercise, where each group first develops a "bad" idea, then moves on to "flip" another group's bad idea, and moves on again to the next easel pad to "flip" another group's bad idea.)
- What are the five most critical benchmarks, milestones, and metrics that will provide you and management with confidence that your Marketing Plan will be a success?

While those questions seem a little blind or obvious as written here, you'll find that in the context of a Marketing Plan in a Day session they take on a life of their own—providing your team with important input that will focus and build your MPD in a content-rich and very efficient way.

Build Warm-ups and Workouts into your outline as you think they will make the most sense in terms of process, group dynamics, and as vehicles to build good content. Use them as you need them. We'll give you some examples in the chapters that follow. You might not have time to do every Warm-up or Workout in your session based on your outline and time frame, and that's more than okay. But you should have a range of these session accelerators ready so that you can add, drop, customize, or invent great Warm-ups and Workouts to power your MPD.

How you include these session accelerators, their timing, and their purpose becomes evident as you build your session outline. Depending on the length of your MPD meeting, you'll design and select ones that balance your outline. You're trying to achieve a dynamic process and meet the goals of your session. Warm-ups, in particular, require a longer meeting because they fuel discussion without essentially filling out the Plan. They're especially good early in the meeting to build a positive group dynamic with content that is fun and nonthreatening to anyone. That said, it's always good to have a couple of Workouts in reserve. As the session unfolds, you might find the opportunity to add a Warm-up or Workout that can help the group focus on objectives—especially if the group gets stuck in advancing key issues at any point in the meeting.

# 9

# Power Words

"Abracadabra!"

—ANCIENT ARAMAIC INCANTATION

WORDS MATTER. THROUGHOUT THE DAY, WORKOUTS, DISCUSSIONS, and voting will turn up key words at various points in pursuit of your meeting objective. Use them to your advantage and to build consensus and points of view about what you're doing. When identified as important descriptors, we call these words Power Words, and they reveal your understanding of your business, your customers, and the relationship you have with them. Power Words are consensus words—words generated in the meeting that resonate with a number of people in the session.

For starters, you can ask people to generate key language to describe any aspect of the Plan.

"What five words would you use to describe our product?"

"What five words best describe our customers?"

"Focus our brand positioning in five words."

Or maybe you're having a discussion about your current tagline, "The World's Most Perfect Company," and it occurs to you that maybe there isn't a real consumer benefit in that line. This is a good moment to stop the discussion and ask people to describe, in five words or less, the benefit that customers get from your product or service.

Two things to note:

First, don't tell people (initially) that you're looking for Power Words or even clue them in to the concept of Power Words. It will make them self-conscious and will slow things down. They'll start writing taglines, which isn't really what you're trying to do. You're looking to uncover a consensus around certain ways to talk about your business. Telling them you're looking for Power Words will block their natural inclination to just describe their beliefs. And tell them not to overthink this. Write down the five words that come to mind—not a tagline, not a sentence, just the five best words that come to mind.

Second, we always suggest asking for "five words" or "five words or less." (Paul likes to insist on exactly five words. Steve prefers around five words. We voted. Unfortunately it was a tie.) If you don't limit people, they'll write a treatise and stuff every conceivable marketing message into their statement. Five words seem to give people enough room to write something meaningful but not so much that they can just scribble away. (You'll be amused by how many never-before-hyphenated words emerge during the exercise in an attempt for people to cram extra content into the five-word limit.) Focus. Focus. Focus.

Here's a list from a recent workshop:

6

## BRAND PROPOSITION

**Gives a sense of discovery**

The same performance . . . for less

Perfect alternative to the expensive option

Great quality at low price

Right combination: quality and price

Great results and price, accessible everywhere

Good quality relative to price

Delivers significant price

Note that several people went to six words. No one was shot. Yes, we aim for five, but we don't get compulsive about it. (Paul does . . . but, in this session, it looks like Steve won the vote.)

There are a couple of ways of deriving Power Words. One way is simply to discuss and highlight the words that appeared to emerge as Power Words based on the exercise. What words seem to have power? What words did multiple people use? As you can see from the example, certain words found their way into multiple people's submissions. In our example, *quality, performance,* and *price* were

6

## BRAND PROPOSITION

### Gives a sense of discovery

The same <u>performance</u> . . .for less

Perfect alternative to the expensive option

Great <u>quality</u> at low <u>price</u>

Right combination: <u>quality</u> and <u>price</u>

Great results and <u>price</u>, accessible everywhere

three words that got multiple mentions. The facilitator can simply note these and underscore them on the easel pad.

Another way to get at Power Words is to have everyone vote for five words independent of their original submissions. Tell participants to forget about their specific contribution and to consider all the words on the page to vote for the best words. Underline the selected words. Add numbers as superscripts to those that receive more than one vote.

Now you want everyone to do the exercise again.

The first time around, you got their top-line, gut reaction. Now that they have the reveal on Power Words, they're going to be even more focused and judicious about the words they choose. And you'll start to get a clear picture of how your marketing group thinks about your brand. In the repeat exercise, instruct participants to select any of the Power Words they want as well as to use any other words that might come to mind. They will be freer in their thinking, but more strategically focused in their five-word selection because they now have a sense of the group and what matters most.

In the repeat of the exercise, the phrase "Combination of Quality and Price" was written by three separate individuals! And the words *quality* and *price* were on virtually everyone's list. Clearly, their team had a strong sense of shared vision as to the brand's strength. And a great point that served as a focus and rallying cry for the rest of the session. By leaving that phrase on the wall so everyone could refer back to it, they had a touchstone against which all the rest of what they did could be evaluated.

Keep in mind that you're not aiming for a tagline. Leave that to the people you work with (partners, vendors, etc.) who have that expertise. You're looking for a set of words that will help to focus everyone's thinking for the day. In the above example, had we been doing the session at Walmart, they might have come up with "Combination of Price and Value." As a tagline, it's not that impressive. Converted into "Save Money, Live Better," it has a consumer-oriented value proposition that sums up the idea (and ideal) of "Combination of Price and Value." No, our session was not with Walmart, but their tagline shows how they incorporated value into their consumer proposition to advance the business from solely a price proposition (e.g., "Always Low Prices"). So even though your five Power Words may not land on the ideal brand positioning or rallying cry, they'll certainly give you the direction and focus you need to move your entire Marketing Plan forward.

Enlist Power Words and voting for any range of issues and topics where you need precise language to focus your Plan. Tally your results. Post the scores on the wall for everyone to see and for ready reference during the meeting. Again, don't worry about not reaching Nirvana language in the session. There will be plenty of time after the MPD to easily fine-tune your go-forward language.

# 10

# Your Vote Matters

"I do not agree with what you have to say, but I will
defend to the death your right to say it."

—VOLTAIRE

ALL OF US HAVE GONE ALONG WITH THE MAJORITY EVERY ONCE
in a while, but no idea in history was ever unanimously approved.
("Gee, General Custer, do we really want to ford the Little Bighorn
River?") Throughout the session you're going to develop ideas, initiatives, programs, prospective partners, or other dimensions of the
Plan that are worth prioritizing. Some exercises may prompt or inspire multiple ideas or possible initiatives. When you're faced with a
range of opinions, options, and points of view, voting is a great tie-
breaker and prioritizer.

## Marketing Plan in Action

A retail manufacturer had a Marketing Plan in a Day session in
which they listed fifteen marketing programs they thought were
important. Even without an actual estimate, they knew those fif-

teen items would exceed their marketing budget—not to mention their personnel capacity for taking them all on—for the fiscal year. By asking the seven attendees to vote, they were able to get a clear picture of which items everyone thought were the most important, easily and efficiently. As a bonus, they knew what they had to budget for in the following fiscal year.

Voting always brings out the truth of what's under discussion. If you have a disagreement over strategy, tactics, messaging, media—almost any area under discussion in the MPD session—you'll find that voting clarifies where you want to go. It's quite amazing. It always works! Voting will provide snapshots of group consensus and offer important truths along the way. Use voting as needed and often throughout the day. Use the right kind of voting for the right situation and you'll focus the will of the group and dramatically streamline the meeting.

## SHOW OF HANDS

The simplest voting technique is the classic one: a show of hands. Fast. Convenient. It's the easiest way to tally up answers once you've gotten everyone to write down their answers or if you don't care whether someone's vote might influence others in the room. (As absurd as it sounds, there are still plenty of people who want to go along with the group.) Show of hands is the fastest way to get a quick read on the group consensus. But if you think people might be influenced by others' votes, then have them write down their favorites first and then use the show of hands as a tally. (Or, to keep everyone honest, you can always collect the votes.)

## PRIORITY WEIGHTING

Priority weighting is the technique that identifies priorities for business focus. It can be implemented to help sort a wide variety of issues, including company strengths, new initiatives, budget allocation— just about anything where it's critical to create focus that will direct prioritized action. This technique can be accomplished with a show of hands or a closed ballot, but it's a more refined technique.

For example, let's say you've identified six brand strengths:

10

**BRAND STRENGTHS**

Category leader

National distribution

Long battery life

Good pricing

Memorable logo

Great brand name

Ask your participants to prioritize all six strengths, with number 1 representing the greatest strength and number 6 being the weakest brand attribute.

Tally the scores as you go. In the example above, three of the six people in your session might have listed "Category leader" as the brand's number 1 strength. Then "Good pricing," "National distribution," and "Long battery life" got one number 1 vote each. Keep adding everyone's ranking until everyone's vote is tallied on every strength. Your final list would look something like this:

10

## BRAND STRENGTHS

Category leader 1,1,1,2,2,5

National distribution 1,2,3,3,3,4

Long battery life 1,3,4,4,4,4

Good pricing 1,2,2,2,3,3

Memorable logo 4,4,5,5,5,6

Great brand name 5,5,6,6,6,6

Total all of the rankings for each strength attribute. Your sheet will look like this:

10

## BRAND STRENGTHS

Category leader 1,1,1,2,2,5 = 12

National distribution 1,2,3,3,3,4 = 16

Long battery life 1,3,4,4,4,4 = 20

Good pricing 1,2,2,2,3,3 = 13

Memorable logo 4,4,5,5,5,6 = 29

Great brand name 5,5,6,6,6,6 = 34

Remember, the strength with the lowest total is the number-1-ranked strength. Reenter the reordered strengths on a new easel sheet. This will be the "hero" strengths page and a key reference sheet as you work through things like your SWOT (Strengths, Weaknesses, Opportunities, Threats) exercise.

As we said, priority weighting is a hugely effective tool for finding out what your collective truth is for any number of your marketing needs. It enables everyone in the room to literally "weigh in" on their perspective on priorities. What comes out the other end is the

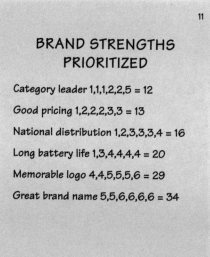

will of the room, the consensus of the stakeholders for go-forward communication, focus, and action.

## STICKY SITUATIONS

We listed small, sticky dots or stars in your list of tools. If and as situations arise, have people vote for ideas by walking around the room and applying the stickies to the item(s) on the pads that they are being asked to vote on. (By the way, the color doesn't matter. Don't worry about whether someone has multiple colors and someone else has only one color.)

11

## MARKETING TOOLS

Web site

Brochure

Trade show

Sales brochure

Leave-behind

TV commercials

Sticky voting is best when there is a large number of items on the wall, you can't do all of them, and you care only about a yes-or-no answer. Rule of thumb: Give people stickers to cover about half the items on the wall. Every idea can have only one vote per participant. If a participant wants to vote for fewer ideas than their sticker allocation, that's okay.

For example:

A retail marketing group identifies ten different projects it wants to undertake. Those projects are spread out over two sheets and have been under discussion for a half hour or more. Things are getting a little heated: Some people are championing their pet projects,

11a

**MARKETING TOOLS CTD**

Package redesign

Showroom redesign

Shopping Network

Twitter campaign

others aren't so sure all the items are that important. It's an ideal time for sticky voting. Tell everyone to pick the five items they think are most important and put a sticky next to each.

Making them choose half of the alternatives will cause some pain and force some hard choices. People will suddenly get thoughtful about their precious stickies. They've got limited resources and must allocate them carefully. Tell them to trust their gut and sticky the ideas they care about. It's easy. But it's also very interesting how voting turns all your people into CMOs.

After they've put their stickies up, total the votes and list each item that got a vote in descending order from most votes to least:

Voilà. There are your marketing priorities for the coming year (or more). It's a definitive list of what your group feels is important to spend your money on—and the order in which they should spend it!

In the coming days or weeks you can ask your appropriate staff groups, partners, suppliers, and vendors to estimate the cost of the various elements . . . and then decide which of them you can afford to do and on what timing.

### Marketing Plan in Action

At a Marketing Plan in a Day for a consumer packaged-goods manufacturer, the meeting attendees voted for eight different new

media alternatives out of a field of nineteen communication vehicles generated through a brainstorming process. They were able
to go straight to their media partners and ask for a budget range
for each of the eight. The cost estimates came in at between $1.65
million and $1.95 million—enabling them to develop a fully inte-
grated workable Plan for their $2 million budget.

Sticky situations are particularly good for new product development. After you've spent half a day coming up with a huge list of line
extensions and new ideas, there comes a time when you've got to
focus on the best projects. Sticky voting is a powerful way to get
everyone to put up or shut up. In a matter of minutes you'll know
where everyone wants to focus their energies.

So make voting part of your MPD mix. It's your right. Use it often
and wisely and you'll get a clear focus on your needs and objectives
every time.

# 11

# Put Up a Parking Lot

"There is no time like the present for postponing
what you ought to be doing."

—XANDER'S PRINCIPLE

START THE SESSION BY PUTTING UP A PARKING LOT. IT'S OUR
term for an easel page that stays up on the wall near the moderator
for the entire day. Title the page "Parking Lot" and explain its purpose to everyone.

During the meeting, ideas will hit the table that are notable, contentious, interesting, enlightening, problematic, enigmatic, promising, or inspiring. They'll also be off-purpose. But they will be important ideas worthy of further consideration that people will want to discuss. Let them touch on the subject matter, explain why they think the idea is relevant, then add the item to the Parking Lot and move on.

Don't put a page number on the Parking Lot unless you generate so many ideas that you need more than a single page to capture them. At the end of your session, the Parking Lot will be an appendix in your final PowerPoint deck.

Don't restrict the Parking Lot to the Leader. Make it clear that at any point in the meeting any participant should feel free to grab a marker and add a submission to the Parking Lot themselves. It's a way to capture good ideas without impeding session progress. That's what the Parking Lot is for. It's the place where you can write down important thoughts for care and consideration at a future date.

The Parking Lot is an important tool that lets you keep control of the meeting and stay focused and on time. Parking Lot issues can be major or minor. They can be small asides or huge problems or opportunities. It doesn't matter. But putting them aside (for the moment) is an important way to keep going.

## Marketing Plan in Action

At one MPD session a creative director suddenly thought of a smart way to redesign the company logo. It was an off-meeting/off-agenda idea (not unusual for a creative director), but everyone agreed that it was an intriguing idea and a possible opportunity. It got added to the Parking Lot so that no one would forget about it.

At other MPD sessions we've seen new product ideas, strategic alliances, line extensions, and other initiatives mentioned that were off topic at that point in the meeting but highly relevant to the business for later in the meeting or another day.

The following Parking Lot is typical of what you'll see for a session: miscellaneous notes and asides that need to be dealt with by the organization.

As you can see from their Parking Lot page, as that MPD session unfolded, it was clear to that team that their Web site wasn't pulling its weight. They needed to reorganize the architecture of the site so that it could accommodate their new direction.

They also saw the opportunity to create a new holiday mailer that could catch their target audience at a time when they would be receptive to the company's message. Again, not specifically germane to the meeting objectives but important to the brand.

Finally, they recognized that the company leave-behind no longer matched their messaging. So a reminder to redesign it went straight onto the Parking Lot to be addressed in a future meeting.

As you conclude the session you should review the Parking Lot pages together, ask if anyone has any additional items to add, make sure everyone understands all the issues, and maybe even assign

## PARKING LOT

- Web site—new architecture

- Own/create relevant holiday outreach/mailer

- Redesign leave-behind

players who will be responsible for advancing each of the Parking Lot issues. You may well find that the Parking Lot will lead to future MPD sessions. This is not uncommon. A Marketing Plan in a Day session is a lot like life: When you deal with one unsolved problem in an organization, other related opportunities may arise. Keep the Parking Lot close by and keep the session moving. It's a terrific tool for making sure that everyone's concerns, issues, and suggestions are captured without losing sight of the goal or goal line.

# 12

# In Session

"Effective leadership is putting first things first.
Effective management is discipline, carrying
it out . . ."

—STEPHEN COVEY

NOW YOU KNOW THE TOOLS. USE THEM WELL AND YOU'VE GOT
control of the session and your company's future! A brief review and
further explanation:

## THE OUTLINE

This is your guide to getting the right things done in the time allotted. Put it together the way you put together a crossword or jigsaw or Sudoku puzzle: Start by putting the easy things in first. And by "easy," we don't mean "Meet and Greet," and "Introduce Yourselves." We mean the things you absolutely know you need to cover.

From there, you back up and fill in. Ask yourself the question, What will we need to uncover in order to address these topics? Ask yourself, What Workout would best address specific topics? If you think you're going to have an engaged, participatory group, you probably won't need many Warm-ups, but you might want to have two or three: one to lead off the session, one for the morning break, and one after lunch. The idea is to keep the participants engaged, the content advancing, and the collaborative spirit growing throughout the day.

When you've got your preliminary outline done, edit and reorder it to ensure that the logic of the meeting makes sense. Then put timings against each item. When you're in the actual session, you'll have to decide whether to let certain things run longer or cut them off. You may even decide to reorder content as the meeting dictates. But by having the outline in front of you (and only you), you'll have control of the clock.

## THE EASEL PAD

As the Leader, the way you manage the easel pad determines how you manage the session. In case we didn't make this crystal clear, here's the real simplicity of the MPD:

The Plan is written on the easel pad. It's a record of the meeting content. As the session goes along, page by page you'll be building out the Marketing Plan with the help of the entire room. Leadership is focused by your clear and visual connection to the easel pad.

The Leader should capture every outline element explored, including content from Warm-up or Workout exercises.

Each page has a title.

Each page has a number.

If a topic runs more than one page, make sure you title the second and third pages of that topic with the same title, and use letters

(11a, 11b, 11c) to indicate that these pages are continuations of the same topic (and as recognition that each of these topics represents one slide in the Plan).

## IT ALL UNFOLDS ON THE WALL

As discussed in chapter 1 (Place and Space), good wall space is critical to the planning session. You'll want three good walls (four is better) that can accommodate your sticky easel sheets. It's quite likely that the Plan will literally fill the entire perimeter of the room. There is something utterly satisfying about being surrounded by the Plan you create.

The importance of the adhesive pad pages—okay, we'll make one more try for a lifetime supply of free Post-it pads—is twofold. First, you want to be able to post the Plan notes quickly, easily, and on any wall surface (e.g., wood, wallboard, glass, etc.) in sequential order around the room. Second, you want to be able to easily move the note pages as the Plan takes shape and some pages become reference for other material or as exercise pages turn into appendix content right before your eyes.

Each sheet is a slide in the Plan. Numbered and added to the wall, they provide a glimpse of what the final PowerPoint Plan will look like. The numbering is critical because when the entire meeting is done, you're going to stack those pages together from number 1 to the end. You'll have those later in your office to refer to as you compare it with and edit the PowerPoint (chapter 33, Wrap-up/Follow-up). Sometimes information gets added or thoughts get expressed that aren't captured as clearly as they can be by the person recording the meeting onto the laptop. Saving and referring to the original notes is vitally important in ensuring that the PowerPoint presentation is identical to or clearer than the easel pad pages.

## POWERPOINT SCRIBE

A computer stenographer—the PowerPoint note taker—is a critical player in the room. This role is a great opportunity for an up-and-comer in your organization. She gets to witness the power of the planning process, the development of the Plan, and be a part of the meeting. But her task and focus is to accurately record the Plan, not to contribute to it. Ideally, the Leader will work in advance with the note taker to provide a PowerPoint template for recording the Plan. This isn't critical but can be helpful for the note taker to know the scope and direction of the day's events and likely elements in the Plan.

That said, the note taker needs a clear view of the Leader and the easel and should record everything written on the pads (and sometimes make note of sidebar comments the Leader may want to revisit later). She needs to understand that the planning process is dynamic. Sometimes new slides will need to be inserted and some outline items may not surface during the day if the group dynamic moves into areas not previously discussed.

The note taker should have permission from the Leader to interrupt the group in order to clarify content to be sure that what is being recorded is an accurate reflection of both the Leader's and the group's intent.

At various break points during the day, it will be beneficial for the

Leader and the note taker to compare notes to be sure that the Plan being captured in PowerPoint is consistent with the Plan developing on the wall. When the session is over, the Leader is going to have— and should absolutely take—the original pages to compare and edit with, but your life will be a lot easier if the person doing the recording gets the notes right in the first place.

### Marketing Plan in Action

When we do an MPD we generally like to have both Paul and Steve as active participants in the session. But at one MPD session with a dot-com start-up, we had Steve doing the PowerPoint recording. At an early break, Paul went over to see what Steve had recorded—and was surprised to find that the PowerPoint pages had very little in common with what Paul was recording on the easel pads. It seems Steve was making "executive decisions" about what was being said and writing down what he thought the company should do with the information. Paul politely reminded Steve to "just write what's on the wall." He's subsequently been promoted to Excellent Note Taker.

## COLORED MARKERS

Multiple colored markers will enable content to be highlighted for emphasis or for tabulations of voting. Underlining key phrases or words or circling back to key issues in different-colored ink helps emphasize important issues and helps the key ideas jump off the page. You want to have a number of markers to ensure that you don't run out of ink—the Leader will be doing a lot of writing!

At the end of the day, make sure the Leader takes all the easel pad pages as well as the PowerPoint recording of the meeting before he or she leaves the session.

If you understand how to use those tools, you'll have control of the session, control of the day, and control of your business. You'll be able to keep the session moving and build out a working Plan . . . in less than a day.

# 13

# Make 'Em Feel Welcome

"Any time you enter a room, you're either included or
intruding."

—WERNER ERHARD

IF YOU'RE THE FACILITATOR, GET TO THE SESSION SITE AT LEAST
forty-five minutes before everyone else. If you're working off-site
and the session is set to begin at 8:30, get there by 7:30. Make sure
the off-site planning people know you'll be there by then.

Review the space and make sure you've got all your tools. Set out
a name tag in front of each seat. Mix up the players. Give seating a
little thought (but not as much as you did for your wedding). Make
sure each person has a pen, index cards and/or sticky notes, and a
notepad at their place. You can give them stickies and/or stars, too
(or you can hold them back for the surprise element of sticky voting
that may occur later in the meeting). Sprinkle some toys or other
hand candy around the table. Pipe cleaners are always good.

Determine where you're going to stand and where your easel will
be. It should be visible to everyone in the room and easily accessible.
You should stand where you'll be able to make the best eye contact

with all the participants without turning your back on them when you take notes. It should also be easy to tear the pages off your easel and stick them on the walls as you go.

Finally, get the food out and the coffee going. Make sure there's a good smell of something cookin' or coffee brewin' to greet your attendees.

## MEET AND GREET

Welcome everyone personally when they arrive. Give people a chance to get comfortable and set up at their seats. Encourage them to enjoy breakfast. Allow for a half hour of eating and chatter before starting the formal session. Food is love. And free time before the formal start of the meeting is a valuable part of team building.

### Marketing Plan in Action

Every minute is valuable time in a Marketing Plan in a Day. In one session we encouraged the founder of the company to tell the story of what inspired him to start the company—while the rest of the team was eating breakfast. There was an informality and spontaneity to the moment that streamlined some important content and made him much more accessible to the group throughout the day.

When you're ready to begin the session, invite everyone to take their seats, and remind them to turn off their computers, cell phones, iPhones, and BlackBerrys. Let everyone know where the bathrooms are. Then it's time for introductions.

Go around the room and have everyone introduce themselves. Start with yourself. Even if everyone in the room knows you, tell them your name, your job title, and what you do in the company. Also add in some personal note of interest that is either relevant to the task at hand or completely extraneous. Possibly a little humor, if appropriate.

After you've introduced yourself, go around the table and have everyone do the same. Ask everyone to add their own "note of interest" to their introduction. It serves to break the ice and put everyone on an equal footing. If the assistant manager and the CEO are both introduced in exactly the same way, it levels the playing field and signals that, for purposes of this meeting, everyone is equal.

Remind everyone why they're here, how long the session's going to run, the approximate time of the breaks, and what they can expect to accomplish in very general/neutral terms. Let them know there's a plan, maybe hold up the outline, but reaffirm that they don't need to worry about it—that's your job. Their job is to be engaged, to participate, to be candid, to listen, and to build the Plan collaboratively as the day progresses.

Write "Parking Lot" at the top of the first sheet on your easel pad. Explain its purpose and invite anyone to add items to it throughout the day. Tear off the Parking Lot sheet and stick it on the wall where anyone can add to it. Then grab your outline and let the session roll!

# Part Two

NOW YOU KNOW HOW TO PLAN AND IMPLEMENT A MARKETING Plan in a Day session. The next part of the book addresses the topics and territory you'll need to cover.

This is the content phase of what will be in your outline and your finished Plan. The next three sections go into depth on how to get the answers to the critical three questions:

1. Where Are We Now?
2. Where Are We Going?
3. How Will We Get There?

This structure is strongly recommended because it expresses in very simple terms the territory you'll want your Plan to cover. It demands a beginning, middle, and end. It will discipline your Plan to unfold like a story and to have a resolution that's both satisfying and action-oriented.

The chapters included in these three sections are guideposts. They discuss and drill down into the key outline topics that will likely populate your Plan. They're not sacrosanct. Remember, every Plan is different. Every outline is specifically customized to your task. So these chapters should be read, viewed, and reviewed as helpful and logical structural pieces to help shape the foundation of your individual Plan. Always keep in mind that this is your Plan, your blueprint, your unique architecture for the idea you are going to build and put into the marketplace.

So read on. What follows will inform your outline, your session, and your very satisfying Plan result!

## SECTION THREE
# WHERE ARE WE NOW?

IT'S IMPORTANT TO GET YOUR BEARINGS BEFORE START-
ing out on a journey. Even a GPS needs to know where you
are before it can give you directions. This section is about
bearing down on the business issues your group needs to
confront before you can build a solid foundation for your
Plan.

This section will address questions about your marketing
vision, your company mission, and your brand positioning.
We'll discuss your competition and larger competitive frame
and examine the intriguing question of what business you're
really in.

Completing this part of the Plan will set the stage for the
decisions you're going to make going forward. It serves as
the foundation on which your Plan will be built. It will help
set in motion initiatives and actions that will be more efficient, more fun, and lots more successful.

# 14

# Why Are We Here?

"Don't bunt. Aim out of the ballpark. Aim for the company of immortals."

—DAVID OGILVY

NO MATTER HOW MUCH YOU'VE PREPARED FOR THE MEETING and explained its purpose, we guarantee that some people will show up clueless. They'll show up with their own plans, schemes, agendas, schedules, annoyances, and distractions. As the session facilitator, your task is to get everyone on the same page as quickly as possible.

So what are the first questions to ask yourself (as you prepare the outline) and your team (as you start the session): What do you want to achieve? What's your goal? What's your objective? For both the meeting and your business. (You'll be amazed at how varied the responses can be—the people who've set their meeting sights too high, the people who haven't given the issue much thought, or the people who may disagree.)

## MEETING OBJECTIVE

Start by making sure everyone is in agreement about the objective for the meeting. Chances are the group you've assembled has never articulated business goals to one another. Everyone assumes they're in sync in their approach to the business. But it's quite likely that the group isn't on the same page both in terms of the business and the goals of the day. To make sure everyone is pulling in the same direction, we suggest that you open the meeting with a simple Workout:

## MEETING PURPOSE (WORKOUT)

What's the purpose of the meeting?

Have everyone take an index card and fill out the answer to that question. We think it's important to have everyone write down their own answer rather than just asking the room. If you ask for answers out loud and your CEO is the first person to speak, no one's going to disagree with him. Having people write down their answers helps to uncover the different points of view. Ask them to keep it short, but to be specific.

Now go around the room and have everyone read what they wrote (e.g., "Get a clear vision of where we're going"; "Set a plan and budget to achieve next year's sales goals"; "Confirm product lineup to determine next year's sales goals").

Write each submission on your easel pad (and do a quick check to make sure your note taker is with you and capturing everything verbatim).

Our examples above are all pretty much in the same ballpark. They focus on getting a handle on next year's sales goals. What you want to do as the facilitator is generalize or synthesize what your people write and put a clear, concise statement on your easel pad.

Sounds easy, but it won't always be. Believe it or not, there will be sessions that start with some disagreement about purpose. You might have to use your Parking Lot right off the bat. Or you might have to spend a bit of time getting one or two people in alignment. Don't be impatient. Chances are they've got the same interests and concerns at heart; they just may feel that other priorities should be addressed first.

It's our experience that people who write different meeting objectives on their index cards are really in agreement—they've just jumped ahead to a different part of your outline. For example, you asked them to write the objective and someone's addressed the issue of methodology: "Develop a new tagline."

But that's a process, a tactic, a deliverable, not a meeting objective. And it's just a part of the larger objective for the day. Listen closely to the objective statements and bring them into agreement by acknowledging what everyone wrote and make them feel comfortable by telling them that all their issues will be covered later in the session. Feel free to synthesize what each person wrote and draw the group to a common objective.

*Don't move on until everyone in the room is in agreement. Remember, consensus is the high ground of what the Plan will achieve, so agreement on what you're looking to achieve for the day at the outset sets a foundation for what will follow.*

And once you've accomplished that objective of setting a clear objective, you will have the skill set to be a jury foreperson—so don't try to get out of jury duty next time; you'll be an invaluable asset to the courts.

Review what you've written on the easel pad and make sure everyone signs off on it. Then write the number 1 on that sheet of paper, tear it off, stick it on the wall, and dive into the meat of the session.

## WHAT'S THE BUSINESS OBJECTIVE?

Are we asking the obvious? Don't be so sure. Getting at the business objective is about the pursuit of truth. It's the reason you do everything you do. You'd be amazed at how many people in business or life slide over this critical starting point.

*"Sell more widgets."*

No, sorry, not specific enough. How many more widgets? To whom? Where? Over what time frame? You've got to drill down to a granular level here—and there's an excellent chance you're going to find some surprises. People may not have pinpointed the specific objectives for their department, brand, or business. But there's no way the day's work can be accomplished if the purpose and the business reason for being aren't shared by all participants. No common objective, no consensus, no Plan.

The simple question is: What do you want to achieve? Is it about starting a new business? Introducing a new product? Increasing sales? Developing a new promotion? Creating a new advertising campaign? Devising a dynamic new media plan? Uncovering new marketing partnerships? Do you want to be more successful? More powerful? More independent? More compelling? All of these? This is important stuff.

### Marketing Plan in Action

At one Marketing Plan in a Day the CEO handed in three different index cards on a simple brand mission Warm-up exercise. That company obviously needed to extend their Warm-up into synthesis-building work so the CEO could land on a single purpose for her business and a consistent elevator speech to describe her business's reason for being.

Another session produced an angry exchange between the CEO and CFO about what the objectives were. Suddenly, a light went on in the CMO's eyes. For the first time in the two years he'd been working at the company he understood why nothing his team did ever got approved on the first go-round. The revelation made it much easier for him to navigate management with future initiatives and recommendations.

You can see why it's important to get all key business stakeholders to the MPD meeting. This little commitment of time can be a huge cost- and time-saver for the future.

## BUSINESS OBJECTIVE (WORKOUT)

Have everyone write down (on an index card or sticky note) what they believe the business objective of the company is. One objective. One goal. Written in an economy of words.

Go around the room and ask each participant to read what they think the business objective is. Capture all those answers on another easel pad sheet.

Now review all the answers. Are they in sync? Does everyone know what the business model truly is?

When you've finished the Business Objective Workout (and don't be surprised if this takes upward of a half hour or more), everyone should have a clear idea of how you got to where you are, as well as where, in fact, you are.

# 15

# The Vision Thing

"The best way to predict the future is to invent it."

—ALAN KAY

AT THIS PART OF THE MPD, THE VISION THING ISN'T ROCKET SCI-ence. It's a stake in the ground, an educated guess, and an informed business dream. Where do you want to go from here? Why? How are you going to get there? Over what period of time? Who is going to make it happen? What's the endgame for the stakeholders? What's the pot of gold at the end of the rainbow? It's about imaging and imagining the future so you can create the future.

No one can see the future, but you can make an educated guess. And, truth be told, if all you're going to deal with is the present, then you're always going to be playing catch-up or worse.

How many business plans have you seen that account for a future recession? And even when the future is predicted accurately, many businesses don't plan for the worst or even for a rainy day. Four-dollars-per-gallon gasoline was predicted by a number of people ten years ago. But most car companies were caught flatfooted when it became a reality.

Making an educated guess about where your business can go isn't mumbo jumbo. It isn't magic, either. *It's your job*. It's what they hired you for in the first place. No risk, no reward. Hard work, tough analysis, and savvy connecting the dots can enable any of us to look forward and assess what *can* be. You need to do that in an annual Plan, a three-year Plan, or a five-year Plan.

Business vision is an art. It's shaped by ideas that are rich, resonant, and radiant. There are often big, gaping holes in a marketplace that can be filled by an inspired idea that's well executed and well communicated. It's no accident that more than several business founders and CEOs who conceived of robust brands and entrusted them to next-generation management have come back to take the helm of their businesses. A great business vision evolves, but it doesn't fundamentally change. And when the next generation loses sight of that vision, the company strays. Many articles and books— good and bad—have been written about Steve Jobs and his management—good and bad—of Apple. But none of them ever claimed he was a lousy visionary. Someone's got to have that vision thing; otherwise you've got a rudderless ship, a pilotless plane. And if no one else in the company is articulating it and driving it, it had better be you!

## SAY IT PROUD

The business vision isn't a long-winded, lofty statement. Save that for the mission statement. Actually, your mission statement shouldn't be long-winded or lofty, either, but we'll talk about that in chapter 16 (What's Your Mission?). A good business vision should be a single idea expressed clearly, compellingly, and uniquely. It's the extraordinary standard you hold yourself and your company to. Some reach for the BHAG. What is your Big Hairy Audacious Goal? Now, that's a vision! It needs energy. It needs reach. It needs aspiration to the next level. It needs future focus. It will be refined as a brand positioning, but for the moment you should use it as the statement that distinguishes your business and business goals.

### Marketing Plan in Action

We started an MPD session by asking everyone in the room to write down what they thought was the vision of the company. Before reading their answers out loud, Steve asked the CMO if she thought everyone had written down the same answer. She just laughed and said, "No bet!" Articulating the vision is one of the first opportunities you have to make sure everyone is on the same page.

If you've got your vision, great! But if you think the company's direction is unfocused, you can try a Workout or two to get on the way.

## BENCHMARK BRAINSTORM (WARM-UP)

Identify a brand you really like and respect. Brainstorm the business vision that drove its success. Each participant writes down the business vision in seven words or less. Record all submissions on the easel pad; discuss and edit if you want to spend any real time with this. The point is to loosen up people's thinking and get them out of the day-to-day box of "what we're doing now" and into the landscape of *"what are our possibilities?"*

## FOUNDING VISION (WORKOUT)

Have everyone take an index card and describe what they believe to be your company's business vision in seven words or less. Record all submissions on the easel pad, then discuss and edit to land on the vision that drove, is driving, or will drive your business. Is everyone excited by it? Great! That should tell you that you're on the right track. Is everyone comfortable with it? Even better! That means the team can rally behind your plan for where you should go. But if there's some discomfort, find out what it is. Most of the time it comes from people who don't think the company can deliver on the promise. If that's the case, park that thought in the Parking Lot and note it as a long-term project for you to rally the company internally.

## CASH-OUT VISION (WORKOUT)

Amend/edit the founding vision into a perfect marketing situation in five years, ten years, twenty years—whatever you decide. Focus on the business endgame, cash-out, earn-out, or pass-along. Are the same seven words (or fewer) that were at play in play? What's the size of the business? How will your customers perceive the company? What will the cash-out be? What will you need to do to make that vision happen? How much money will you make?

Don't be surprised at the intensity of emotions that comes up in this Workout. We cautioned you that the business objective and vision were going to be tough pieces of the strategic puzzle. The people in attendance have just laid out a serious, ambitious, but achievable road map for your organization. Possibly for the first time since the company was founded.

Wow!

Food for thought. For disagreement. For conversation. For common understandings. For dramatic consensus. In fact, this is probably a good place for a quick coffee break. But let's keep going . . .

# 16

# What's Your Mission?

"A mission statement is a dense slab of words that
a large organization produces when it needs to
establish that its workers are not just sitting around
downloading Internet porn."

—DAVE BARRY

A MISSION IS A CAUSE. IT'S WHAT YOU STAND FOR. WHAT YOU
fight for. It's a statement of the business you're in, the beliefs you
hold dear, and the way in which you fulfill what you do. It's also your
description of how you want your customers to see you. It's a plaque
on the wall in the reception area that tells everyone who walks
through the door who you are, what you do, how you do it, and for
whom you do what you do. It's also your vision delivered . . . and
more. If vision is the BHAG—the elegant, aspirational goal—then
mission is the comprehensive statement of that goal that encompasses all your stakeholders.

Got a mission already? Terrific! Is it complete? Does it embrace
all of your constituencies? Is it working for you? If so, good for you,
great, move on. But time and again we see that mission statements

tend to be lofty ideals that are disconnected from the actual business of the company. A great mission statement should be organic and integral to the way you work. It should be the kind of statement that gets a nod of affirmation and a feeling of pride from every employee every day.

If your team is on a roll, you might not need a Warm-up. But if they're still struggling to articulate the company's vision and mission, you could try a Warm-up that helps to build their imagination and storytelling abilities. Something like this one:

## THE DRAMATIC STORY (WARM-UP)

Think of action-film plots: *Raiders of the Lost Ark, Transformers, Armageddon, Star Wars, Batman.* Invent a new story. Make it rich, deep, dark, perilous, fun, funny, dynamic, dramatic, out of this world . . .

- ✓ Who are the key characters?
- ✓ What do they have to achieve?
- ✓ What are their key impediments?
- ✓ Who are the adversary characters?
  - ✓ Why are they bad?
  - ✓ How can they be overcome?
- ✓ How will the good guys triumph and achieve victory?
- ✓ What will victory look like? What's the happy ending to the story?
- ✓ Will there be a sequel?

Whether you've used a Warm-up or not, this is a key point to address the actual mission:

# THE REAL MISSION (WORKOUT)

In a single sentence, write down the key statement that will drive your mission. What are the methods, commitments, business beliefs, and core values that make you special? In several sentences, what is the purpose, direction, and means to achieve your objective? What's the nature of the business you're in? Who are all the constituencies you serve? What makes you special in the way you serve your audiences?

Select bullish players who are enthusiastic that they've nailed it. Write their mission statements down on the easel pad. Ask for additions from the room. Entire thoughts or, better, additions and build-ons. Look for language/words that add to the mission idea, propel it, engage it, empower it, and enrich it.

### Marketing Plan in Action

A business school started to refocus its mission with a Workout that turned up the following building blocks:

## MISSION STRENGTHS 6

- Urban and suburban locations
- Ability to get things done
- Co-op and career services
- Quality internships
- High-quality business world experienced full-time and adjunct faculty
- More personal attention to students
- Close relationship between faculty and students
- Care about student outcome

The follow-up to this Workout was a smaller group of people who synthesized the language into a comprehensive mission statement.

This could be a good time for a Power Words exercise. You've got a lot of language on the easel. Lots of building ideas, but likely no holding line that expresses the entire mission of the company, business, product, or initiative.

## POWER WORDS (WORKOUT)

Give everyone five votes. Go through every word on the easel and record the number of votes it gets. Publicly ask for everyone to vote for what they believe are the most important words and record the number of votes each receives. The most popular are the Power Words. Underscore and capture the number of votes each one gets.

Then challenge the group to write their mission statement again . . . on an index card. There are no restrictions on what words they may use, but the Power Words can guide them. And the deliverable should cover the following:

1. Business definition
2. Customer commitment
3. Employee promise
4. Ethical stance

Depending on time, collect their statements and read them, record them on the easel pad—and then move on.

Do you need to do all this mission statement building? Well, that depends on your company, your situation, and your objective for the meeting. Remember the only things you have to address are, Where are we now? Where are we going? and How will we get there? If you're thinking about, rethinking, or developing your mission statement is important, then add it to your outline. If you think it isn't, don't include it. Again, it's totally up to you.

Our own belief is that a mission statement isn't really an important part of any business or marketing plan. (Really? Did they really just say that?!?) Actually, we did. There are two things you should know about a good mission statement:

1. It should be integral to the company. A mission statement shouldn't be a goal, it should be what the entire organization eats, breathes,

lives, and sleeps. As we said at the start of this chapter, it's really just the vision delivered. It should drive every aspect of the company's processes. It should be built into every fiber of the business and every move the business makes. As such, it's not an "add-on" or an "after-thought" or a "good idea." If you don't think the company can or does live up to its mission statement, it's time to write a realistic one.

2. The mission statement isn't part of your Marketing Plan. It informs and frames everything you do, but it exists over and above and outside the Plan. A mission statement is more of a summary or touchstone. It's the pledge and the plaque, not the Plan.

Reflecting on what everyone wrote on their index cards isn't important—unless the purpose of your meeting was to write a mission statement. Otherwise, just collect all the index cards, write the thoughts on an easel pad, and save them for later on to be reviewed, tinkered with, edited, and wordsmithed. This is an exercise that propels your session. The final language of your mission statement will take time and should be written and refined outside the meeting!

### Marketing Plan in Action

A New York–Hollywood production company was moving into the new digital landscape. They did a Marketing Plan in a Day and developed a clear messaging list, but they ran out of time before they could write the mission statement. A few days later the CEO took a stab at it and sent what he thought would be an innocuous e-mail to all the attendees (the other officers of the company) with the two-sentence mission statement he was going to post on the Web site.

What ensued was a firestorm of e-mails back and forth among

the five passionate attendees. Everyone weighed in on the state-ment indicating what they thought was right or wrong about it—but all of their comments were based on a shared knowledge of the ses-sion and the goals of the company. It took two days and approxi-mately thirty e-mails (times five people cc'd on each) before they all could agree. But when they did, they were extraordinarily happy with the final statement. The CEO sent us an e-mail wryly commenting on what he thought was going to be a simple note, but he admitted that the final statement was more encompassing, more user-oriented, and a better expression of what their company could deliver.

A good result, but note to selves: If we had made the MPD a bit longer than the four hours we allotted, we could have saved lots of back-and-forth e-mail and nailed the mission statement collabora-tively, in the meeting.

So do some thinking about whether your company's mission needs attention. If it does, then make room in the day for this very worthwhile discussion.

Now is a good time for the facilitator to assess the room. Are people feeling the love and landing on common high-ground agree-ments? Or is there some tension or disagreement about mission? Can you pick a Workout from your toolbox (or make one up on the spot) that can build consensus? Ideally, you've gotten everyone in agreement and talking seriously about your company or organiza-tion's situation, heritage, vision, mission, and perspective.

If you're all moving forward together, it's time to take a hard look at where you fit in the mind of your customers and the eyes of your competitors.

# 17

## Positioning: Who Are You?

> "'You!' said the Caterpillar contemptuously. 'Who
> Are You?'"
>
> —*ALICE IN WONDERLAND*

YOU KNOW WHERE YOU WANT THE COMPANY TO GO. YOU THINK YOU
know what your business is all about and probably think you even
know why your company should be a big success. It can happen.
Provided you tell the truth to yourself and your customers about
who you are. Exactly. Briefly. Uniquely. Completely. Compellingly.

Positioning is about helping your customers understand why
they should care about your products or services. It's about helping
them understand where you fit in on the landscape of possible
choices.

Positioning is about brand/company/personal identity. (We tossed
in "personal" here because a Marketing Plan in a Day can work for a
freelancer as effectively as it can for a Fortune 100 company.)

Positioning is about focusing on your reason for being. About
ensuring you don't get mired in an identity crisis or, perhaps worse,

a squooshy, fuzzy-wuzzy, nonleverageable description of who you think you are or who you might like to become.

*Without a crystal-clear and distinguishing position, you have no shot of building a workable Plan, let alone a successful business.*

There's been a tremendous amount written about brand positioning. Read any and all of the source material you want. The caution here, though, is that so much of what has been written about positioning complicates the issue. We're about keeping it really simple—really challenging, but really simple.

First, ask yourself whether you need to address positioning in your MPD session. At the very least, you should probably reiterate it during the session for everyone who's there. But you might need to build it over from scratch or fine-tune it. If so, read on.

In general, a good positioning answers the following four questions:

### 1. Audience

Who is our target—and how do we know that? Just because you want a particular audience doesn't mean you've got it. CBS wants young men from eighteen to thirty-four years of age. They've got a much older, more female audience. Make sure your product matches your ambitions. Wishes are not results.

### 2. Benefit

What unique and meaningful benefit does my brand extend to my customers? It's been called many things. Rosser Reeves made it famous in the early 1960s with his "Unique Selling Proposition" (emphasis on the word *unique*). But it's still a smart point of view.

What's the number one benefit customers will derive from your product or service? Is the proposition meaningful and compelling?

### 3. Rationale

What tangible and intangible support is there for our customers to believe about, care about, and embrace our brand? Also known as the "reason to believe." What reason do people have—especially in this cynical age—to believe anything you have to say about your products or services? Think carefully before you answer.

### 4. Ownership

Can you own the positioning? (Hint: If you can take your company's name off your marketing materials and put a competitor's name next to the line, it's not an ownable positioning.) Also, is it a claim your customers and your company's practices will allow you to own? If you claim "Number 1 in customer service" and you close your customer service line at 4:00 P.M. EST, or you send customers through a phone tree that ends up in an outsourced country where English is a second or third language, then it's not really an ownable positioning.

When it comes to writing down your positioning, don't be lazy. Don't let people write down "good quality at a low price" or "afford-able and best in class." As Gertrude Stein once observed, "There's no there there." Again, refer to our ownership point: If anyone else in your industry can say it, then it isn't worth saying. There's one exception to that rule: If anyone can say it but no one is saying it, then you have the opportunity to "own the positioning." Yes, that seems contradictory to our caveat about an interchangeable positioning, but in this era of parity (or parody) products and copycats and knockoffs, sometimes the unclaimed high-ground claim can be a powerful position to own.

But before you surrender to that, reach higher. Reach for originality and see if you can put a stake in the ground that extends an unparalleled truth about your company. You've got to push the group to think about and write what's truly unique, credible, and ownable. And in the best of all possible worlds, as an exercise you'll borrow a page from BMW ("The Ultimate Driving Machine") and do it in five words or less.

## POSITIONS YOU ADMIRE (WARM-UP)

Pick a brand you admire, respect, or use on a regular basis . . . any brand. What does that brand stand for in five words or less?

More often than not you'll find that the brand you select defies conventional wisdom—the vision of the brand is bigger than the original perception or deliverable of the business. The positioning is bigger, too. Consider Amazon. Most people thought Jeff Bezos was in the online book business. But his vision was much bigger, and every time new merchandise was offered at Amazon.com, people were surprised. But Bezos didn't name it Amazon for nothing. His idea from the get-go was to create a huge online department store. And years ago, when his CFO was asked what Amazon won't sell online, her response—without missing a beat—was "concrete or water." And the only reason she said that was because of the weight of both relative to their shipping costs.

So if you need to identify a strong positioning statement, here's the time for a Workout on the topic.

## WORD POSITION (WORKOUT)

What five words uniquely and meaningfully define your company/ business/idea?

This isn't easy. But here are some helpers: Don't worry about the five words forming a complete sentence. Don't look for the five words to sound like a selling line or slogan. Just identify five words that when strung together uniquely and compellingly characterize your brand. Don't overthink this. The strength of the exercise is in all the content submitted, not your single effort to land on the perfect five words.

Record all the submissions on the easel pad. Compare and contrast them. What are the similar touch points? Where are the departures? Talk about them. Pick at them. It's probable that none of them will be perfect. (If one is, please promote that person to head of marketing immediately.) Remember, this is hard work. The search for the simple is an arduous task. It's the old Blaise Pascal line, "If I'd had more time, I would have written a shorter letter." So here's how to use the task to get closer to the Nirvana position—it's time for another Power Word exercise.

## POSITIONING POWER WORDS (WORKOUT)

Have all the participants liberate themselves from what they wrote on their index cards. Have everyone forget about the positioning five words they wrote in the preceding Workout. Have everyone focus on selecting the five great words on the easel that are most relevant to and compelling for the brand.

Now go through every word on the page and underscore the words that get votes, then place the number of votes above and to the right of each word.

At the end of the exercise, write all the Power Words on a new easel sheet in rank order. Let people react to them. Discuss. And now it's time to do the positioning again.

## POSITIONING: ROUND 2 (WORKOUT)

Do the five-word exercise again. All words are on the table: words from the first round, Power Words that were identified, new words that pop into your head. Encourage everyone to come at the exercise as if they hadn't done it before. But of course everyone has the benefit of the earlier thinking and they'll be closer to nailing the position. Label an easel sheet "Positioning: Round 2" and once again record all the submissions.

You should be a lot closer to hitting the position now. Likely, one of the submissions will be really close. But at the worst, one of three things will happen:

1. You've got it—Eureka!
2. You're close—some discussion and tinkering will get you there . . . or a piece of enlightened synthesis from the facilitator or a participant may get you there.
3. You're not feeling it yet—in which case put the exercise aside and move on to the next place in your outline. You can come back after a break, some other discussion, or the following day to get to the elusive positioning that is close at hand but not quite fully formed at this point in the meeting. Or you can task a smaller

group, the facilitator, your agency, or other interested, objective parties to retool the words to land on the optimal statement. Not to worry, you're likely close enough to an ownable position that the rest of the meeting can progress well.

### Marketing Plan in Action

Working with a packaged-goods company that was introducing a new product line, the team found themselves focusing on four words (three concepts): *clean, pure, price,* and *value*. They landed on a two-word positioning that was a synthesis of those ideas. Later on, their PR firm developed their two-word campaign line and they're still using it two years after the session.

If you're not close to a positioning that everyone feels bullish about, you may have a more serious issue—and chances are it's related to our first four points in this chapter. Either you haven't identified your audience, your benefit, your rationale, or the question of ownership.

If you're not agreeing, take a few minutes and discuss each of those points in turn. Does everyone agree on the audience? Do you know for sure? We've found that frequently someone in the group thinks you have two or three different audiences and he can't decide which audience the positioning should reach. Remember, you can't be all things to all people.

Does everyone agree on the benefit? What about a reason to believe? Do you even have one? This is tough because a lot of companies steamroll ahead on autopilot without providing their customers with that important rationale. Do you know what it is?

Finally, is it ownable? Usually, disagreement about this isn't the reason you can't nail the positioning. But it's helpful to look at when you analyze why you're not able to reach agreement on a position.

Sorry. We wish we could tell you this was easy. But do the hard work. Now. Because if you don't solve or surround your position here, it's just going to keep coming back and biting you on the you-know-what again and again. You will spend untold amounts of time and money chasing a business proposition that is too amorphous to be profitable.

# 18

# Who's the Competition?

"The ability to learn faster than your competitors
may be the only sustainable competitive advantage."

—ARIE DE GEUS

IT'S GREAT THAT YOU KNOW WHO YOU ARE AND WHERE YOU
want to go, but knowing who (or what) is in your way may be even
more crucial. Ask the team to consider what the barriers to your
success are. How will you overcome the various obstacles? Who are
your competitors? Competition comes in all shapes and sizes. Leave
no stone unturned in assessing who or what can be an obstacle to
achieving your business vision and goals.

## COMPETITION: LET ME COUNT
## THE WAYS

There's no such thing as no competition. Sure, your idea is brilliant
and (you believe) very well insulated. But all ideas must have a place,
and all new ideas must achieve a *replace*. Place is the real estate that
you occupy in the minds of your customers as well as the location of

the sale. Replace is the behavior your idea will inspire when you get people to abandon the brand they're currently using for your new and better idea.

In confronting competition you need to identify the category you operate within. That definition is critically important. If you set your competitive frame too wide, you'll get hopelessly lost in a sea of confusion. Who should you target? How are you going to compete? How many aspects and attributes of the customer experience do you need to—can you possibly—fulfill? If you set your category definition too small, you run the risk of "owning" a category with diminishing returns.

Such was the case of the Shake 'n Bake brand years ago. It dominated the seasoned-coating-mix category. Enjoyed a share of market north of 70 percent. But the business shrank right in front of their eyes. The brand was blindsided when meat extenders (e.g., Hamburger Helper) and quick-serve restaurant takeout (e.g., Kentucky Fried Chicken) deeply cut into Shake 'n Bake's business. Their category share remained unchanged as their business tanked. The changing competitive marketplace had not been taken into consideration.

Business changes. Consumers change. The marketing environment changes. The competitive landscape changes. The category you occupy today may be refined or redefined tomorrow. It's no great thrill to be king of the mountain if you're standing on top of a molehill.

And if you think a ten- or twenty- or thirty-year-old packaged-goods example isn't relevant, then you don't truly understand the nature of marketing (which is really human nature). When Microsoft was fighting the U.S. government's antitrust case, Bill Gates testified that he thought Linux was his biggest potential competitor. His statement was met with contempt by prosecutors who thought that the Linux share of market was too small to be a threat. In the meantime, no one was paying attention to Google. After all, it was just a search engine. But the confluence of search and broadband penetration changed the rules in just a couple of years, and even though Congress sneered at the thought that Microsoft would have competition, Google's growth turned out to be a real threat.

And while we're on the subject of Google, let's also talk about *their* competitive frame. If they had tried to launch as the diverse business model they are today, they would have been an abysmal failure. People wouldn't have known what Google was or why they should use it. But Google launched on a very simple, very elegant platform—a search engine with a powerful new algorithm. They were able to express to their customers what they were and what they could be used for. It was only as their model started to get traction that they looked at exploring a wider competitive frame by looking at their proprietary algorithm and asking themselves what the real business was that they were in. And today as their model expands in so many directions, people still refer to their business incorrectly. The genius of Google and its algorithm isn't search, it's *find*! Google offers the most reliable way to access information you seek. So powerful, in fact, that Microsoft now chases Google (not Linux) with Bing and the introductory joke about the name as an acronym for "But It's Not Google."

Keep those examples in mind as you look at your competitive set. You might have to retrench or reset your competitive objectives in order to regain traction or build new and expanded traction. Then look to roll out a new model as you get brand permission from your customers. You want good and serious competitors. They make you better, give you more incentive to market smarter, and provide a bigger market in which you can grow bigger.

What category are you playing in? Ideally, you don't want to exceed 15 percent to 25 percent of that category—tops. Being the dominant player in a small category gives your business nothing to reach for. You need to be able to stretch, maneuver, and evolve to grow. If you own 40 percent to 50 percent of your market share, congratulations. But also shame on you for not looking for a bigger pond. Take Coca-Cola, for example. They've got a huge share of the cola market. But rather than just stay there and fight off competitors like Pepsi, Dr Pepper, and RC Cola, they reached for a higher target. Today, Coca-Cola views water as their number one competitor. As far as Coca-Cola is concerned, they want to be the brand of choice whenever anyone on the planet has a thirst to quench. They recognize how many quarts of beverages consumers drink in a day. And they are in a share of stomach battle. So they might have only a small share of the world's fluid market, but so what? They've now got room to grow.

So who are the other players in your business? Who's bigger than you? Who's smaller? Where do you fit in? How do you expect that pecking order to change over time?

Beyond identifying the players in your competitive frame, who is best in class? What are the characteristics and attributes of best-in-class brands in your category? What distinguishes them? What drives their leadership? Identify the optimal category attributes. Write them down. Rank them from most important fo least important. Evaluate how you stack up relative to the best.

Who are the worst players in the category? What makes them weak? How will you avoid falling into their pitfalls? How will you take advantage of their failings to drive your success?

## COMPETITIVE THEFT (WORKOUT)

Think of something your biggest or best competitor does that really upsets or inspires you. They do it so well that it has—or might have—a negative impact on your business. Steal the best from the competitor: What is it? Why is it so good? Now apply it to your business and make it your *own*!

## COMPETITION, NOT COMPETITORS

The unseen enemy is usually more daunting than the adversary you can identify. Competition beyond branded competitors (did someone say Hamburger Helper and KFC?) may be even more insidious than competitors you can name. The run-up in gas prices in the first decade of the twenty-first century created a far bigger competitive threat to the SUV business than any branded competitor. Competition morphed beyond obvious competitors to the wider world of transportation—more efficient cars and alternative transportation, including trains and buses. Outside forces toppled an entire category of automotive products. Crossover began to make sense. Small became beautiful. *Hybrid* became a happy word.

What are all the possible sources of competition for your business idea? Think carefully, completely, creatively. What are possible issues in the economy, the environment, or the ecosystem that could adversely impact your brand or marketing program? Is your idea in step with—or, better, a step ahead of—customer behavior? Will you be relevant and compelling tomorrow and in the years ahead?

Does your brand name have strong forward momentum? Or are you like castor oil—an effective product with a bad name and a terrible taste? Is your price point attractive relative to the marketplace and other price pressures on customers? Do you represent a value and a value proposition—whether premium or price—that is compelling? Does your brand proposition resonate and rise above not only current competitive offerings but all the external impediments that could derail you? Identify all the "unseen" competitive factors and assess how they can be overcome.

As the facilitator of your session and the builder of your outline, you've got to do some serious strategic thinking here. Before the session, as you're building your outline, talk to your Planning Partner (chapter 3, Every Leader Needs a Partner). How well do you think everyone knows these issues and agrees on them? Will you have to drill down? Will you need a participant from your in-house or vendor research team? Will you need to break your competition portion of the outline into smaller bites? The rhythm of an MPD ebbs and flows depending on what your team knows, doesn't know, or needs to know in deeper, richer, more probing ways. You've got to make some decisions as you build your outline—and be prepared to spend additional time, and skip or add elements, as you get the temperature of the room and the critical issues that will best propel the Plan.

# 19

# What's My Line?

"When I let go of what I am, I become what I
might be."

—LAO TSU

NOW IT'S TIME TO FOCUS ON THE PRODUCT. THAT'S RIGHT, THE
product, not just the brand. What's the difference? The product—or
product line—is the physical manifestation or service deliverable of
the brand. It's what the customer pays for. It's the sum of satisfactions and offerings that fulfill the brand promise. And it damned
well better be in sync with your customers' perception of the brand.
That's the essence of "brand permission": Does the deliverable (the
product or service) have the same characteristics (value, quality,
price, category, etc.) as the customer's perception (the brand)? If
so, great! If not, you've got some hard work to do. Either on the
brand, the product, or both.

As you create the outline for the session, you've got to stop here a
minute and ask yourself whether the product line helps or hinders
the marketing. Does the messaging match the product? Does one or
the other need to be fixed, redefined, or realigned?

Some questions you could ask yourself or talk about with your Planning Partner:

What's included in your product line? How many products or services are in the line? What are the various price points? Where and how is your product manufactured, produced, delivered? Does that matter? How is the line packaged? Where is the product line sold—or where do you hope it will be sold?

Remember, this is a one-day Marketing Plan, not a product development, manufacturing, or distribution discussion. All of those elements in the brand mix are critically important (remember to use your Parking Lot). But as the facilitator, you'll want to have a good working knowledge of that information in case the conversation goes in that direction.

Getting a fix on the shape and range of the product line is important at this stage. The breadth and depth of your line has a crucial bearing on every other key variable in your market strategy—marketing budget, marketing program, brand messaging, communications platforms, seasonality, and sales programs all depend on knowing exactly what your product line is and does.

## PRODUCT LINE PARAMETERS

There are several rules of thumb in outlining your product line. Here's your simple checklist to ensure you're fulfilling your brand promise in the products you extend to your customers:

✓ Does the product line—and every product within it—fulfill the brand promise?

✓ Does the product line offer a complete complement of the products customers expect from your brand?

✓ Does the product line offer a strong complement of attractive price points to power customer usage and loyalty?

✓ Is the product line easily accessible to your customers?

Consider Best Buy as an example of a brand that beats competition because it does a good job at delivering these product line parameters. Best Buy promises and delivers consumer electronics at the best prices. Why go anywhere else? Their product line offers a complete range of hardware and software for consumer electronics and entertainment products. The product line is accessible to customers in at least three critically important ways:

1. Number and proximity of stores
2. Online shopping, loyalty/rewards program, and online consumer communication
3. Service—both in-store and in-home installation. Geek Squad was actually a business acquisition for Best Buy and a very important one because electronics without setup and operation is at best a frustration and at worst a reason to go elsewhere. Remember The Wiz? Well, that chain eased on down the road. Or the fading fortunes of Circuit City? Service is a critical dimension of technology.

So what are you going to do? One of the easiest ways to get at your product line is to benchmark: What have the other guys done? This might be the perfect place to do a Warm-up we talked about back in chapter 8 ("Warm-ups and Workouts").

## INDISPENSABLE WEB SITES (WARM-UP)

Name your three most indispensable Web sites besides Google, Facebook, and YouTube. Why are they essential to you and how did they get that way?

This is a good exercise to get a dialogue going on brand promises, brand benefits, and brand deliverables. It's personal. There are no right or wrong answers and people tend to feel passionately about the Web sites that complement, if not guide, their lives. Google is our go-to location for search. Amazon may be our go-to online location for book buying. But beyond the obvious sites, drilling down through your top three—or even five—Web sites always reveals very interesting niche sites people love for their sports, hobbies, and special interests. Discussing those sites, their brand deliverables and consumer interest in them becomes valuable in getting at the idea of brand passion. Why are those sites so indispensable to your team . . . but your own site isn't on their list? You don't have to embarrass anyone here; this is just food for thought. What makes a brand, a product, or a Web site indispensable?

## FAVORITE BRAND (WARM-UP)

Name your favorite brand or business and the key attribute of that business that makes it so great. Terrific. Now list the key products and/or services in their line that fulfill the brand promise. Why are all of those products key to the success of the brand?

This exercise will get you a little closer to your brand because it moves beyond simple or single brand deliverables into a complement of the brand products, benefits, and touch points that define the brand.

## BEST COMPETITOR (WORKOUT)

Name the best brand in your category (other than you). What are the key drivers for that brand's success? What products fulfill the brand promise? Why are those products the right selection? What makes their offering complete?

The discussion that will ensue from this exercise should take you directly into the products you will or should offer in your brand proposition. What products or services should you include? What was the essential shape of your line at launch or currently? What products should you add over time? What should be the timing for your additions to the line offering? What are the costs? The risks? The rewards? The distribution? What's the incremental profit opportunity? What is going to give you competitive advantage and insulation?

## COMPETITIVE WEB SITES (WORKOUT)

Analyze your competitors' Web offerings. Select one, two, or three of your best competitors. Go to their Web sites and analyze the brand offering as represented on the site. Do this exercise collectively or divide into groups.

You can learn a lot from how your competitors display their brands on the Web. How do they treat their brand name? Their logo? Is there a copy line describing the brand? How is the home page organized? What's the content priority? What does the site map look like? What's the order of items in the site map? What's the tone of the site? How are the graphics? Is the site easy to navigate? And, most important, what are the insights and takeaways for your brand and for your Web site?

This one's a Workout because we're often amazed at how many companies don't keep a watchful eye on their competitors. If you think about it, every one of your customers is aware of and is being pushed to your competitors' sites. Your customers probably know much more about your competitors' offerings than you do. If so, you'd better catch up with them in a hurry.

### Marketing Plan in Action

A life insurance company did an MPD exercise where they selected three of their leading competitors' Web sites as a group exercise. They visited all the sites live in the meeting and opened discussion about the strengths and weaknesses of each. In a low-interest category, they found that one site offered a very colorful game that was great fun, but then led to a high-pressure, very boring selling site. Another site was so busy with content it was impossible to know where to look or what to do. A third provided graphics and engagement on topics that provided a useful, personalized assessment of life insurance needs without the high-pressure sales pitch. Guess which site best resonated with the group? Guess which site invited the longest visit? Guess which brand is doing best in the marketplace?

The question of your product line and its resonance with the brand is crucial to the long-term health and success of your business. While we said at the top that the Marketing Plan in a Day session isn't the place to dive deep into product development, if you feel it should be part of your outline, then don't leave this portion of the session until everyone feels very comfortable about the vision and direction of the company's offerings. But once you do, it's time to build an honest evaluation of the situation. It's called SWOT, for Strengths/Weaknesses/Opportunities/Threats. And it's nothing to be afraid of.

As a tool, a SWOT analysis can be painfully honest. And as a place in the Marketing Plan in a Day, it bridges the Where Are We Now? and Where Are We Going? sections. So depending on your timing, you can put in a break either before doing your SWOT or afterward. Because either way it's time to move on to the next phase of the session, which is: Where Are We Going?

# SECTION FOUR
# WHERE ARE WE GOING?

LET US POINT THE WAY. OR, BETTER YET, HERE'S WHERE you get everyone pointing in the same direction. It starts with the classic SWOT analysis (except we've modified it in two very critical ways). Once you've done a strategic assessment, you'll begin to zero in on the capabilities of your brand by focusing on what you do well. Once you all agree on what you do best, then heading for the finish line will be easy, enjoyable, and exciting.

# 20

# Houston, We Have a Problem

"No one ever went broke underestimating the taste of the American public."

—H. L. MENCKEN

IS YOUR BUSINESS RUNNING SMOOTHLY? BE AFRAID. BE VERY AFRAID. Business today is dynamic and ever changing. Whether you're a Fortune 100 company or a neighborhood mom-and-pop, you're facing changes and challenges in every aspect of your business every time you put the key or electronic pass in the front door.

In taking a good and realistic view of your business situation, you've got to be willing to turn over every stone. Yes, some slithery, slimy, disgusting things will turn up, but that's your job. And once you've slain the dragon(s), there's nothing ahead but a corner office, a soaring stock price, and your picture on the cover of *Forbes*. (Would that it were so simple. But "slithery, slimy stuff" seems overstated, too! Steve wrote that.)

What's your business picture from every angle? What do you need to know, think about, and anticipate? Answering these questions requires a detailed analysis of your situation. To drive opportunities you need to evaluate vulnerabilities and risks as well as rewards.

## HALF FULL OR HALF EMPTY

The optimist looks at the world as if his glass were half full. The good marketer looks at the world to figure out why the glass is only half full. That means you've got to look at the dark side and anticipate problems so that they can be dealt with and averted. That's where a good SWOT analysis comes in.

The Strengths/Weaknesses/Opportunities/Threats analysis is classic marketing. But too many people tend to isolate rather than relate the four components. We also don't like the order of the words. While SWOT might sound cool and easy to pronounce because the vowel is in the right place, the better way to do your analysis is SWTO—Strengths/Weaknesses/Threats/Opportunities. Threats most logically follow weaknesses. They are more easily revealed in concert with weaknesses, which in turn are logically analyzed by turning threats into real opportunities.

So pardon our obnoxiousness, but in this chapter we're going to talk about SWTO. Don't despair about pronunciation. Call it Sweet-O—maybe that will make it sound better, and done well, your analysis will be! And in the MPD there are a number of ways to get at this analysis without exhausting an entire day (or more) undertaking a cumbersome exercise.

The SWTO analysis is one of the most abused and misused analytical tools in marketing. Most marketers don't bother with it at all.

Or if and when they do, they have at it in a shotgun way—identify a few Strengths, some Weaknesses, several Opportunities, and throw in some Threats. It's like ingredients without a recipe. A SWTO analysis is only as good as the discipline that guides it.

Simple principle number 1: For every Strength there is a Weakness, a Threat, and an Opportunity. The process and structure of the analysis should be parallel. The strong SWTO is led from the Strengths. If there are no Strengths, there is no business and no business Opportunity. Which is a very quick way to call the game and regroup before spending a lot of time and money.

### Marketing Plan in Action

At one MPD, we asked the participants to come up with all the business Strengths they could identify in advance of the meeting. At the start of the SWTO exercise, we asked for and captured all the Strengths on an easel pad. We then prioritized them. We then divided the session into three groups to have each of the groups drill down on Weaknesses, Threats, and Opportunities. When they came back together, each of the groups reported and we recorded their input to fill out the SWTO exercise. It was quick, engaging, and efficient.

But whether the SWTO is done in advance of the meeting or in the meeting (much preferred if you can spare the half hour), start by identifying and then prioritizing brand or business Strengths.

## SWTO BENCHMARK (WARM-UP)

If your team is uncomfortable with the idea of starting with your brand, then get them talking about another brand they really respect. No risk, no wrong answers, no pressure. Have everyone scribble down on their index cards what they believe are the unique Strengths of that brand. Record them on the easel pad and discuss what makes these characteristics leverageable Strengths for your business.

## SWTO STRENGTHS (WORKOUT)

Have everyone write down as many Strengths as they can think of for your brand or your business. Go around the room and record them all on the easel pad. When there are duplications, record two hash marks after the first entry to confirm the second entry for the same idea. Keep going around the room until all Strength suggestions are exhausted. If the list is good and complete, call it. If anyone in the room believes there are Strengths missing, challenge the group to flesh out the list.

Now prioritize. All business Strengths are not created equal. Some Strengths are much more important business drivers than others. It's important to get at that relative Strength among Strengths.

Let's say, for example, you've identified six Strengths. This is a good place to use Priority Weighting voting. The most powerful Strength should be ranked number 1, down to the least important Strength ranked with the lowest number. Now you've got a handle on the first part of the SWTO analysis.

## WEAKNESSES AND THREATS

No business is bulletproof. No matter how powerful or invincible a business or brand may seem at any given moment, there is always kryptonite of some kind waiting in the wings. A good SWTO will identify the obvious as well as random or alien elements that can undo a business.

The balance of the SWTO exercise—Weaknesses, Threats, Opportunities—can be done the same way you just did the Strengths analysis: Have all the participants write down their perceived Weaknesses, then list, rank, and vote on them. Likewise Threats and Opportunities. But there's a far more efficient and time-saving way to get at those other important analytical business barometers. The Speed Sweet-O Workout enables the group to fill out the SWTO analysis in a fraction of the time it would take the entire group to complete the exercise.

## SPEED SWEET-O (WORKOUT)

Once you've collectively identified and prioritized your Strengths, divide the group into three smaller teams. Assign one remaining category—Weaknesses, Threats, Opportunities—to each group. Have them brainstorm their list faithfully following and paralleling the Strengths menu. In other words, the team that's in charge of Weaknesses has to identify a Weakness for every Strength. The team in charge of Threats has to identify a Threat for every Strength. Each group records their work on an easel pad. When this work is completed, each group reports its findings and, with some give-and-take, a bit of conversation, and an addition or two from other group members, voilà, the exercise is done.

Number their sheets in SWTO order (Strengths first, then Weaknesses, Threats, and Opportunities) and add them to your wall next to one another and your final PowerPoint presentation, possibly in an Excel spreadsheet for comparison and contrast.

Done right, you've now got a quickie Sweet-O. Which means it's going to be easy to take an in-depth look at the important part of the exercise, which is the O . . . as in Opportunity!

# 21

# Opportunity's Knocking

"Opportunity knocks, but it seldom nags."

—DAVID MAMET

STRENGTHS? WE ALL HAVE THEM. WEAKNESSES AND THREATS? We all face them. Opportunities? Those are the areas you've got to look at if you plan to grow your business. Microsoft had plenty of chances to enter the search business. But they didn't see search as a powerful Opportunity early enough to dominate the market. Apple had many Strengths, Weaknesses, and Threats. But it was their realization that the music business was in chaos that gave them the Opportunity to create iTunes and the iPod to reinvent the music business.

So where are you going?

Opportunity is the intersection of inspiration and preparation. It arises from your vision of what can be and is grasped by your ability to execute. Think too small and your Opportunities will be minuscule. Think too big and your ability to execute will be overwhelmed. You intuitively know when Opportunity presents itself in the area of new product ideas you want to bring to market. You see Opportunities in new promotions, partners, or entirely new business ventures. It's one thing to see Opportunity—no small feat—and quite another to harness Opportunity into business and marketing success. That part takes discipline and planning.

There's an old expression that the light at the end of the tunnel can sometimes be a freight train coming the other way. Knowing whether you're heading for the light of inspiration and business success or an illusion and disaster requires that you confront and answer a number of careful questions.

You've gotten a good head start in identifying and categorizing Opportunities in your SWTO analysis. But now, beyond just stating your Opportunities, you've got to drill down to give Opportunity dimension. You've got to put specifics—definitions, timing, and numbers—around them. You need to be sure that the ideas will hold up to the many challenges the promised Opportunity has to confront and overcome in the marketplace.

There are some basic issues you've got to address in clarifying your marketing Opportunity. Just as we said about business Strengths, all Opportunities are not equal. Some may be small steps that are smart and right for the business. Some may be momentous game changers that will require more careful thought, planning, action, and investment. The analysis of Opportunity starts with scope and inclusion. What's the size and scope of each Opportunity? And what are the elements included in the Opportunity? More specifically:

## CAPITAL INVESTMENT

What's it going to cost to get into business or advance a new initiative? The answer is always "more than you think." So if you're going the VC route or seeking internal funding, estimate big and bold to make sure the money you raise will enable and empower your idea sufficiently to prove it a winner before you need to go back and ask for additional financial support. What does phase one look like? What will it take to get it up, out, tested, and proven?

## MANUFACTURING

Who is going to make or manufacture your product line? Where? At what cost? How reliable are they? Do they have a vested stake in your success? If you're manufacturing applesauce, who's growing your apples? Your success is their success. How nimble are they? How fast can they respond to and fulfill an order? Do you need multiple vendors to ensure that your manufacturing and service needs are met? To provide flexibility and options should one supplier falter—for any reason?

## DISTRIBUTION AND SALES

Who is going to distribute your product or service? What are the best sales outlets for you? Who is going to comprise your sales team? Lead your sales team? In-house or out of house? What's the sales plan? What's the sales budget? What are your sales incentives?

## PARTNERS

Who's coming along for the ride with you? You will identify key operatives in manufacturing and sales. But who are the other people or companies who can contribute to your success? Promotional partners? Strategic partners? Allied companies? Who out there can help make your marketing budget look and act bigger because they promote your brand in activities and initiatives important to their business? How can you make 1+1 = 3?

Opportunities present themselves all the time. The smart businessperson or team are the players who seek them out, identify them, put them into a Plan, and harness them to drive the business.

## OPPORTUNITY KNOCKS (WORKOUT)

Give everyone an Opportunity category to think about. Or have someone in the group identify an Opportunity area that might be most beneficial to the business. It could be a production Opportunity, sales, distribution, new product, strategic alliance, whatever. Now have each participant come up with a business Opportunity that makes the most sense within the category. Write them all down on the easel pad. Discuss them. Maybe Priority Weight them through voting. There will be good business fuel in that list.

## TIMING AND MILESTONES

When you roll it all up, what will the business achieve in year one? By year three, five, or ten? What does success look like? What milestones do you need to attain and on what time frames to achieve your goals? How will you measure them? What does an exit plan look like? Opportunity is business optimized. It is success that enables you to walk away at some point with significant rewards for the risks you've taken, for the Opportunity you've realized. All of these questions will be answered as the Plan unfolds and in the weeks and months as the Plan is activated. For now, envision what success looks and feels like. And state it as best as you can. It will be the target you reach for and manage against.

### Marketing Plan in Action

In one session we asked everyone to write down what they thought their business would look like in three years, five years, and ten years. How big did they think their business could become at each of those benchmark years? We asked them to focus on key milestones they would need to achieve to drive their business to the next level. And finally we asked them to fantasize about what the endgame might look like. Would the business be big enough to sell? For how much? To whom? This was an empowering exercise that got them thinking about a longer horizon for their business.

From the point of view of your Marketing Plan in a Day session, you've got to ask yourself how important these questions are for this session. Before the meeting think about whether you're ready to even ask them. Or are these questions for a smaller, senior management team to focus on? Is it most appropriate to skip over all this and come back to it in future sessions? Or are the fundamentals of these questions important for all stakeholders to agree on so they're not managing blind but working toward common, agreed-upon goals? Either way, you can't afford to ignore them! The opportunity is too great!

# 22

# I Can See Clearly Now . . .

"We all live under the same sky, but we don't all have the same horizon."

—KONRAD ADENAUER

THINK ABOUT HORIZONS IN NATURE. THEY STRETCH AS FAR AS THE eye can see—in the distance, to the left, to the right. They're seamless, consistent, unencumbered. They're logical, often beautiful, and effortless.

A brand's horizon is its scope and capabilities. How deep are the brand credentials? What does the brand do really well? How far can the brand extend? What are the Strengths of the brand performance? And what is the brand permission—the boundaries the brand needs to respect and stay inside of to remain relevant and meaningful? What are the brand yeses?

Understanding the potential of the brand can open up Opportunities that aren't always immediately apparent. Steve likes to tell the story of the years he worked on the Discovery Communications business. From 1992 to 2000, it seemed that almost every year DCI would buy or launch a new network. First TLC. Then Travel Channel. Animal Planet. The list goes on. But growth was fueled by John Hendricks's vision that Discovery had brand permission to create programming that went far beyond the number of hours it had available. Since the hours of the day are finite, it just made sense to acquire or launch compatible networks. Today, DCI is a multibillion-dollar brand. If they had stayed with only Discovery Channel, they would have been acquired and absorbed long ago. Here, the winning formula was to think outside the network!

So here's a good spot to think about your own potential. And if you need a Warm-up, here's a simple one that can be accomplished in group discussion and/or by having everyone write down and offer up a brand yes:

## BRAND YES (WARM-UP)

Have someone identify a brand they like. Have everyone in the group think about and create a line extension for it—a smart, logical, can-do, should-do business extension.

How easy is that? Advertising executive George Lois told this story years ago in his autobiography, *George, Be Careful*. His agency was working with Aunt Jemima and the company was waffling (sorry, we couldn't resist the pun) about manufacturing maple syrup. The agency's president went out on the street to conduct an impromptu survey, and 25 percent of those surveyed claimed they were already using Aunt Jemima syrup. How's that for a slam-dunk winner? It was so logical that Aunt Jemima could be/should be in the maple syrup business that consumers already believed it was in their pantries.

Here are a couple of other brand extensions that were perhaps not as obvious but became powerful extensions for two well-known brands. Barnes & Noble and Borders bookstores landed in the same place with their partnerships with Starbucks and Seattle Roasters. A coffee bar in a bookstore now seems like a natural. But in the days before Amazon began eating up their market share, bookstores were all about "Come in, buy a book, and get out; don't touch the magazines; don't sit down." Today they both recognize that hospitality and giving people a reason to come to the store is their competitive advantage over Amazon.

Nietzsche said, "What does not kill me makes me stronger." If your competition doesn't put you out of business, it's going to make you better. And for all those who suggested the bricks-and-mortar bookstores would soon be dinosaurs, the coffee shop extension provided an experience online bookstores can't match. So the new model is "Come into my bookstore, read my magazines, have a cup of coffee (and a pastry), and use the weekly coupons I send you so you'll keep coming back for more."

### Marketing Plan in Action

At an MPD training session, we asked the team to take on the issue of brand relevance and brand loyalty. We gave them Blockbuster as an example. Reason to appear is a problem that Blockbuster is struggling with but hasn't yet solved. Why should anyone go to their stores when they can download films or order them via mail on Netflix? Initially Blockbuster added candy, popcorn, and other movie-theater-type experiences, but that hasn't been enough.

And now they've got a major issue to address that won't be solved by a repair as simple as "Get it in the mail, drop it in our store." The training group jumped in enthusiastically and generated more than a dozen ways Blockbuster could build traffic to Blockbuster stores! It was an effective way to demonstrate how group thinking on an intractable problem can often lead to inspired solutions and richer horizons.

Consider Xerox, once the first name in copying. So much so that people didn't make copies, they xeroxed. In a highly competitive office environment Xerox has evolved its business to become a sophisticated end-to-end business solutions company that sells very high-end copiers and digital printers to big businesses and entrepreneurs. A fundamental extension of the Xerox business today is customer relationship meetings and seminars at a beautiful learning center on the grounds of the company's offices in Rochester, New York. These seminars are offered throughout the year at no cost to customers to engage them in making the most of their Xerox product investments. People happily come from all over the country to take advantage of the learning, business, and networking Opportunities Xerox offers. It's a great way for Xerox to drive loyalty and a welcome way for customers to increase profitability with Xerox products. The Xerox "line extension" isn't a product at all. It's a customer relationship education, business optimization, and networking experience!

So with those ideas and examples to inspire (or scare) you, now try it for your own team:

## GREAT EXTENSIONS (WORKOUT)

Put your participants in groups of three to five (or more), depending on the number of people in your group. If there are six or fewer players in the room, have them work individually on index cards. Have the teams work together and come up with the best brand extension idea they can think of for your product or service. The guide points here are that the ideas must fulfill the following criteria. The extensions must be:

- ✓ Consistent with your brand positioning
- ✓ Affordable and achievable
- ✓ Consumer desirable
- ✓ Additive to your brand proposition and profitability

And yes, this is competitive. So once you've generated a list of extensions, write them down and go for . . .

## SIMPLY THE BEST (WORKOUT)

Of the ideas generated, which is the best one? Instruct your players to suspend their disbelief and land on the best idea. Or, if the competition is too fierce or the loyalty to each group idea too intense, do a voting exercise where people can vote for any idea but their own. Focus on the best one or two ideas, depending on the amount of time you want to dedicate to this exercise, and get at why the ideas are so good. You can even drill down deeper here and discuss when in the life cycle of your brand these extensions should be launched and assess the upside they will offer your brand.

We think you'll find these two Workouts really powerful stuff. They go a long way to cutting through the underbrush and identifying true product/service Strengths and Opportunities. Now, if you haven't landed on your positioning from before—and time permits— do the Word Position Workout from chapter 17 (Positioning: Who Are You?) one more time to see if your team can now land on the Nirvana positioning for your offerings.

# 23

# You Gotta Know Your Limits

"I recognize my limits. But when I look around I
realize I'm not exactly living in a world of giants."

—GIULIO ANDREOTTI

YOU CAN'T BE ALL THINGS TO ALL PEOPLE. THERE ARE LIMITS TO
what your brand can do or achieve. What do you do well that no
one else has matched? What do you have permission from your
customer to do? We're talking category relevance and competitive
insulation.

## COMPETITIVE INSULATION

Competitive insulation is a protective mechanism. You want your
brand getting business and profitability from all reasonable sources
of revenue, but you've got to recognize what your brand does really
well and what it doesn't. It's time to confront your

1. Brand capabilities
2. Brand boundaries

3. Barriers to entry
4. Corporate agility

We'll talk about strategic alliances later, but even with the bookstore example in the previous chapter, note that Barnes & Noble and Borders chose to partner with established coffee companies rather than launching coffee businesses that aren't inherent to their core capabilities.

Amazon is in the warehousing and shipping business. What they sell is almost beside the point. eBay is in the online sales business. Auction or fixed price . . . doesn't matter to them. McDonald's is in the restaurant business. Beyond burgers, they've continually expanded their brand with breakfast, chicken, salads, ice cream, and coffee. Having a clear understanding of what business you're in is critical to recognizing the core capabilities that can best extend your product line and profitability.

In your everyday life, you're well aware of things you do well and things you don't. You're great at crossword puzzles. You run fast. You're a brilliant host. Whatever. The things you do well you do often. They give you joy and often get you praise. The things you don't do well you leave to others.

The same is true in business for your brand. Know your brand capabilities. What does your brand do inherently well? Those performance Strengths come directly from the brand positioning. They inform the brand offering. What are the boundaries of your brand? Where shouldn't you go because it makes no sense, it's too risky, too expensive, too unprotected? Knowing your brand shell is important. It will protect you from stupid, costly mistakes. Your brand and corporate agility will take you to new areas of brand strength, reach, revenue, and profit Opportunities. Paying attention to your barriers to entry will protect you so that you pursue only Opportunities consistent with success and cushion you from tough falls from heights you never should have tried to scale.

## THE WORST (WARM-UP)

Get someone to volunteer a brand that had a really terrible brand extension. What's the brand? What's the extension? Why was it a bad idea? What were they possibly thinking? What was the brand conceit and violation that made it so bad?

A good example of a bad idea was when Coca-Cola, in their soft-drink-supremacy cockiness, went into the clothing business. Sure, the occasional Coke T-shirt might have some appeal as a brand premium or even a one-off purchase. But the likelihood of a brand loyal customer base buying an entire wardrobe of soda-pop-based apparel was well beyond the reach or "permission" of the brand.

It's critical to understand what sandbox you're playing in. How big is it? What toys are inside? What fantastic things can you create and build inside your play space? You can't be all things to all people. And you don't want to be. You don't have the resources. Your audience can't or won't embrace a brand definition that exceeds your expertise. You'll find yourself competing with a whole new category of adversaries. And perhaps worst of all, your customers may think less of you for treading where you have no reason to be.

# YOUR WORST (WORKOUT)

Now it's time to think bad thoughts about your brand. It's usually way easier to come up with truly dumb, terrible ideas than struggle to find great ones. The assignment is to come up with the worst brand extension or idea you can think of for your brand. Encourage everyone to come up with really dumb, horrendous ideas. Individually, or as a group exercise, share the horrific ideas, have a good laugh—but then get to why they are so bad. How did you come to them? How do they violate the brand boundaries? What are the lessons to be taken from these bad examples?

It seems counterintuitive. Why is it easier to come up with bad ideas than good ideas? Probably because of the psychology of not looking foolish in front of your peers. The range of bad ideas is limitless. You wouldn't implement any of them anyway. So it's easy to be right . . . er, we really mean wrong. If you start this section by asking the group to come up with the best new product idea for your business, no one's going to say a word. No one wants to offer up an idea that might not be a slam-dunk winner. But everyone feels capable of coming up with a bad idea.

### Marketing Plan in Action

We were doing an MPD at a condiment manufacturer and thought a Your Worst Workout would be a smart way to loosen the participants' thinking. Divided into three teams, the group started coming up with bad ideas. But they just weren't bad enough. "Mint-flavored mustard" might be a little unappealing, but it's certainly not the worst. We stopped the exercise and asked the person who had that idea to make it worse. After a few false starts she came up with "vomit-flavored mustard." After a good (gross) group laugh, everyone loosened up and some really vile and terrible ideas started to appear. Good momentum for the next step of the process.

Once you've got those bad ideas out (and enjoyed a good laugh or two), the next Workout turns the whole exercise upside down:

## THE 180 (WORKOUT)

How could your bad extension ideas be flipped into good ideas? If you have enough people participating, a great way to do the worst and the 180 is as a two-part exercise. Divide into groups and put easel pads around the room. Each group puts a bad idea on the pad. Then have each group move clockwise (or counterclockwise, if you prefer, because there is indeed something seemingly backward about this method) to the next easel pad, where it will confront another group's bad idea. With no "pride of authorship," now the task is to do the 180, turning a really bad idea into a great one. Keep going around the room, having each group react to the bad idea at the top of the page and creating a 180 turnaround to it. It's much easier to come up with a good idea this way. When all groups have confronted all bad ideas, review the work. What did people do to the bad ideas to turn them into good ones? What now makes it a good idea?

Time and again, we find these two Workouts reveal wonderful Opportunities where none existed before. As the members of your team bring their considerable experience, knowledge, and expertise to the assignment, they'll think about your company in new and different ways. The result will probably be some major new initiatives you can develop further in the session or down the road.

## ATTRIBUTE/BENEFIT (WORKOUT)

An alternative to the bad idea Workout is an attribute/benefit exercise. You can start this off individually and then pool the collective

| ATTRIBUTE | BENEFIT | 16 |
|---|---|---|
| Always low prices | Save money | |
| | Live better | |
| Luxury performance | Ultimate driving machine | |

intelligence of the room. Have everyone think of meaningful brand attributes—what does your brand do well? Then have them conceptualize benefits—what are the meaningful customer satisfactions your brand fulfills?

Once you've isolated attributes and benefits, it should be much easier to think of line extensions that fit the attribute/benefit profile and expected delivery of your brand.

But now it's time to move down the road ourselves as we explore the third essential part of your Marketing Plan in a Day . . .

## SECTION FIVE
# HOW WILL WE GET THERE?

IT STARTS WITH THE BIG IDEA. YOU MAY LAND ON IT IN the meeting or agree to the parameters of what it needs to be. Either way, your task will be to agree on your paths to market, the tools you'll use, and the dream team that will activate the Plan. A next step is adding partners (if that makes sense for you), and only then should you start to look at your budget.

Once you've got all these pieces in place, before you pull the trigger you should ask yourself (and the team), How will we determine whether what we're doing has worked? Finally, beyond all the chatter and patter, there's your action plan, timetable, milestones, and responsible parties who have to get it all done.

# 24

# What's the Big Idea?

"Practice safe marketing—use a concept."

—RICK HEFFNER, FUSZION, INC.

WE ATTRIBUTE THAT QUOTE TO RICK ONLY BECAUSE HE'S THE FIRST person we ever heard say it. If William Safire's lexicographers can find an earlier source attribution, please excuse us, and congratulations to the original coiner of the phrase. But we digress.

Welcome to the "How will we get there?" phase of the MPD. You should expect this third section to go faster than the previous two, because by now everyone's on the same page, everyone's agreed on the current situation and the objectives, and everyone will start to organize around the one single, strongest idea that can produce the results you want.

But first you've got to come up with the Big Idea.

If your ad agency people are part of the session, they're going to hate this. Because this is the part where they're accustomed to taking over, to telling you thanks for the brief, "We'll get back to you in a few weeks," at which time they mysteriously reappear with print ads, TV storyboards, a campaign slogan, and a lot of mumbo jumbo about how they had to do voodoo incantations and assign thirty creative teams to come up with the Big Idea. It's about the only thing agencies have left to sell you, and if they see you start to build it out in front of them in a couple of hours, they're going to start to get very uncomfortable. And with good reason. Because they believe one of the last vestiges of their control over the client relationship is that they are the purveyors of the Big Idea.

But the inspired agencies of today—and tomorrow—will welcome this new way of working. After all, a great idea achieved through dynamic consensus of all brand stakeholders will make everyone's life a lot easier. These days, you can't afford to have a vendor relationship with your marketing suppliers. In fact, if you're not willing or comfortable to give your agency a key to your office building (or if they're not comfortable with the idea of you dropping over whenever you'd like), then you need to rethink your relationship. It's all much more dynamic today. Or it won't work.

More and more agencies are assigning staff members to camp out in their clients' headquarters, to be part of the day-to-day action, and to connect business needs to advertising opportunities in a dynamic and seamless process. Your ad agency, PR firm, Web firm, collateral agency—they should all be fully engaged partners and teammates in every way. In these kinds of partnerships the results are greater than the sum of the various moving parts.

Both you and your agency should demand and foster a complete partnership. In other words, have a marriage, not an affair. The old way needs to become the new way. And if good ideas come from you, not them, they should be just as happy as if they had come up with the Big Idea. You're all in this together. At the same time, you shouldn't start thinking that you don't need them. Too many companies hire vendors and start treating them as "fired employees." They ask the vendors to do the work that a former employee used to do (in fact, in many cases the vendor *is* that fired employee). Clients who do this are making a big mistake.

Instead you should be asking yourself what Strengths your organization lacks that a vendor, excuse us, other partner, could provide. Then, as we pointed out in *The Little Blue Book of Advertising*, "Let the people you hired do their jobs." Or, as Mozart was purported to have said to his patron the Prince of Salzberg, "You pay me far too much for what I do for you and not nearly enough for what I could."

Where were we? Oh, right—the Big Idea! Can your team do it? Maybe, depending on their skill sets and who's in the room. But you don't have to land on the perfect, magical set of words in this session. What you might land on is just the single, working expression of the idea that sums up where you want to go. And that's okay.

Now you're on the search for the rallying cry that will keep everyone focused or deliver your message to your customer. Hint: It's not quality and it's not price.

## QUALITY ISN'T A BIG IDEA

Yes, yes, we know it works for Mercedes. But that's the result of a long-term strategy they've been building methodically for years. Did you know that Mercedeses are taxis and police cars in Germany? They're that affordable. Mercedes made a conscious decision early on to export to the United States only models that were fully loaded (as standard equipment) with every luxury feature that's an option every place else in the world. Automatic transmission? Standard. Leather seats? Standard. Power windows and AC? Standard. Strip all the luxuries off a Mercedes and you can use it as a taxi. Except in the United States, where luxury is essential to their brand proposition.

We were listening to an audio CD by Dan Kennedy called *Confidence, Power, Dollars, Wealth,* and he made one of those throwaway comments that stop you—or, at least, us—dead in your tracks. He said that quality isn't a sales hook. That people can't ever really know the quality of your product until they've bought it and used it. Before then, any claims you make about quality are just puffery. We sell on *belief.* The proof of the product or service is in the *experience.*

## PRICE AIN'T A BIG IDEA

Live by price, die by price. It's an old expression that continues to hold true in the marketing business. If you claim to have the lowest price in town, someone's gonna show up with a lower one. The Advertising Hall of Shame is filled with the taglines of sloganeers who claimed to have the lowest price. And you can probably recite some that are still pounding that drum. They may win in the moment, but inevitably a competitor will meet or beat them on price and offer some other differentiating benefit and life will become very difficult. It's been a painful path to reinvention for Toys "R" Us following Walmart's growing presence in the toy business. Toys "R" Us was founded on the warehouse idea of price and inventory. Brilliant. Then. When Walmart met TRU on price and beat them on weekly destination, Toys "R" Us needed to scramble to update its reason for being: Inventory? Environment? Destination? Specialist? Boutiques? Yes. These are all part of the new Toys "R" Us . . . but price is no longer their differentiator.

## SO WHAT'S THE BIG IDEA?

The Big Idea is a concept that communicates the heart of your product or service in a real, credible, differentiating, and compelling way (BMW: "The Ultimate Driving Machine"). It gives people a conceptual and/or emotional experience of the product before they actually try it (American Airlines: "We Know Why You Fly"). It's a call to action, a pledge, and a promise. It connects directly to the customer, not the company.

Think about one of the great ad lines of all time: "Just Do It." Here's a guy in Oregon who's been a track coach for years and had to hand-build his students' athletic shoes because nothing on the market did the job properly. He ends up with an amazing shoe and a whole bunch of patents and goes to a local ad agency (Wieden & Kennedy) and asks them to come up with a campaign. Now, if Nike and/or Wieden & Kennedy were second-rate players, they would have come up with a line like "Better Innovation, Better Performance" or "The Best Sports Shoe. Period." And the agency could say to the company, "See, our positioning and copy line references your patents and talks about what a great shoe you make."

But they were better than that, more inspired than that. And they came up with a line that was directed toward the end user and was the *emotional expression* of every professional and amateur athlete's secret dreams: "Just Do It." Don't worry about being great at it. Just get in the game (or sit by your TV in your Nikes fantasizing that you're in the game). In other words, be a part of the action, be in it, Just Do It. Genius.

Will you hit that kind of home run in your session? Probably not. But what you should be able to do is get to the essence of the idea. The insight underlying the idea is the important goal in the MPD. The killer selling line can come later. So the expression of the idea might be a little clunky, but what you come away from the session with should be the core idea that you're hoping to have your customers think of when they think of your brand(s). Remember, this is the Marketing Plan in a Day, not the Creative Tagline in a Day. And anyway, if your creative people can't land on the killer line, Steve is available to provide it.

## HOW DO YOU FIND YOUR BIG IDEA?

There's a good chance your Big Idea is already up there hiding in the easel sheets. But here are some Workouts that will help you find it.

## HIDDEN IN PLAIN SIGHT (WORKOUT)

By now you probably have ten or twenty easel sheets covered with such words as *exclusive, patented, useful, first, only, transcendent* (please invite us to your MPD session if you've got *transcendent* on your wall—sounds like fun!), and other seemingly ordinary words that describe your product or service. Have everyone take a note card and write down the five most important Power Words they can find on the wall. Paul likes the number five for Power Words.

You'll be amazed at what's hiding in plain sight. Go around the room, and as people give you their lists of Power Words, use a different color marker to underline each word on the sheets. Then tally up how many votes each word got and put those numbers on a new sheet, from most votes to least votes.

Now do it again.

After you've done it a second time, ask people to create a list of Power Words. Now you've got as many as ten or twelve interesting words on the wall. Chances are you can start to put them together in a four- to six-word phrase that differentiates your product or service.

## Marketing Plan in Action

A couple of years ago we did some work with Dial on their Purex brand. From this exercise about five ideas rose to the top. All were brand-viable. Generating them made the group feel creative, empowered, and fulfilled in their exploration. It was then very simple, through discussion of brand positioning, assets, and voting, to get at the two top choices and ultimately the direction the brand initiated: "Purex Saves Green."

It was a double play on saving money and the environment. It was a brand platform they were committed to. It was a brand direction senior management wanted to advance. And it was a brand initiative the PR agency—sitting in the meeting—had already taken steps to implement in publicity outreach. The program turned out to have far more reach in terms of media, trade, product, and customer touch points as a function of the MPD ideation.

It also turned out to cost less and be far more easily executed in the marketplace than if we had not landed on the idea in the session.

The words you've now put together should be your rallying cry. Your Big Idea. *Not necessarily your tagline!* If you want to, you can ask your ad agency, PR firm, or other freelance consultants to offer up taglines that express your Big Idea in a more consumer-oriented or emotionally driven expression. But for purposes of working through your Marketing Plan, you've got the unifying idea that will carry the weight of all the marketing you plan to do.

Think of it as the perfect elevator speech for your next campaign. The one the CMO can present to the CEO to burnish his credentials and demonstrate that everyone is on the same page. The phrase that will be the litmus test of every marketing idea you come up with from this point on.

In fact, that should be your first test of your Big Idea. Does it encompass everything you've already planned to do and everything you're thinking about doing? Does it talk to all your target audiences? Does it embrace every aspect of your company's product, service, and mission? If so, great! If not, go back to those lines you've had everyone write and ask them what's missing. See if you can add or edit a word or phrase that can focus the statement.

Also think about where the idea will live. In today's multiplatform, digital landscape, where are customers likely to see your idea? If that's where they are, that's where you should be. There's serious brainpower in the room. Work it to get at all the customer touch points your campaign should reach.

The Big Idea is critical to everything you're planning to do.

Whether you use it as your actual sales line or give it to others to polish, it should summarize the intrinsic, compelling benefit and value to your customers of what your brand can deliver.

Will it change? Maybe—as circumstances change. But as long as you're clear about your product, audience, and message, it should serve as an anchor for everything you're planning to do. BMW has continued to be "The Ultimate Driving Machine" for every year the car has been marketed in the United States.

# 25

# Follow the Yellow Brick Road

"I have a feeling we're not in Kansas anymore."

—DOROTHY, IN *THE WIZARD OF OZ*

IN *THE WIZARD OF OZ* THE YELLOW BRICK ROAD WAS THE ONE CLEAR path to get to pay dirt—the Wizard. It seemed scary and there were impediments along the way. But the path was clear. (Though getting in to see him was another thing. Ironic, actually, because the truth is never in the Wizard. It's in the bundle of capabilities that reside in you. But again, we digress—or we've just given ourselves an idea for another book.) If only it were that simple for us. If the path to successfully reaching our customers was so clearly delineated and easily traversed we'd all be marketing geniuses.

Paths to market should be viewed as a creative task. How are you going to communicate all of this physical and intellectual capital to your market, your customers? There are many roads to take. Some are going to be much better than others. But there are many, many paths to pay dirt. There will be impediments along the way. But you've got to anticipate them and build them into your Plan.

So yes, go ahead and think Yellow Brick Road. What is the clearest, most logical, most efficient way to get from here to there? Whom do you most trust to get you from point A to point B? Google Maps? MapQuest? GPS? Your mom? Employ that same kind of logic in building out your Marketing Plan. Answer three fundamental questions to provide the direction for the route you will take:

## WHO IS YOUR MARKET?

How well do you know your target audience? What kind of research or media or evidence do you have to support that answer? If you are confident in your knowledge of whom you want to reach, ask yourself where you will most efficiently find them. And in this age of digital media and new platforms addressing diverse lifestyles, it's much more complicated than it used to be. But it's way more satisfying when you land on the paths that are going to most completely connect with your prospects. Think media, lifestyle, buzz, partners.

Levi's once had such a lock on the denim business that they lost their way with a new generation of people under thirty who weren't interested in wearing "their parents' jeans." It's been a long, tough road back ever since. Once again, if you try to be all things to all people, you'll end up being nothing to anyone. Make sure you really know and agree on who your audience is, what they want, how they're evolving, and how you are going to stay relevant and compelling to them at every turn. This is an active and ongoing commitment to your brand—and to your customer.

## WHO IS YOUR TRADE?

Where will your brand be distributed? What do you need to do to get sell-in and support from your sales partners? Don't ever underestimate or overestimate your trade relationships. For many packaged-goods manufacturers, supermarkets still hold a controlling hand in "slotting fees." On the other hand, pharmaceutical companies figured out how to make an end run around the doctors about ten years ago and started advertising directly to consumers—delivering "push" from the end user as well as "pull" from the doctors. Which situation do you face? Is there a way to solve that problem?

And while we're on the subject, don't forget your sales force. Will they need special training for your new Marketing Plan? New materials? Do they even have the skill set to implement your current plans?

## WHAT'S YOUR BUDGET?

Is your budget sufficient to achieve success? Do you have the support you need from your partners? Your company? One of the key values of doing the Marketing Plan in a Day is that your team will clearly identify the priorities and needs of the company. It will serve to make a persuasive case at budget time (in fact, we often suggest people do an MPD just before starting their budget process). It also identifies ongoing needs for months and years ahead. This is too important a question to be left as a paragraph—you'll find a whole chapter on this question at the end of this section. Budget is a fundamental part of the strategic process. Whatever money you spend, make sure it is an effective allocation to meet a specific goal.

## TAKE THE B.A.I.T.

We've created a simple and elegant inventory that can keep you on track. We call it B.A.I.T. and it stands for Brand Action Inventory Task. It's a seven-step process that will keep you focused at this stage or that you can decide to do later. The Brand Action Inventory Task gives you an action fix on your brand. It asks seven simple questions:

1. What's for sale?
2. Who is the target bull's-eye?
3. What is your differentiated benefit?
4. How and when will you make your sale?
5. What is the messaging?
6. What behavior do you expect?
7. How will you build a brand relationship?

Each one of those questions can be a Workout. In fact, B.A.I.T. can be the focus of an entire MPD day or a task for a smaller subgroup to fulfill outside of the MPD meeting (or in advance of it). It's your call on how you want to play it, and it's something you should decide before the meeting based on who is in your session, what the shared knowledge is, and the amount of time you have. Does everyone agree on audience? If not, you might want to do a fish or cut B.A.I.T.

## FISH OR CUT B.A.I.T. (WORKOUT)

Have every person write down the top three markets for your product or service. Tally the votes and rank them from top to bottom.

You might not want to do seven separate Workouts, but doing a combined seven-question Workout can be complicated. You'll have to pick the key questions to keep your particular session going. What we like to do is put the B.A.I.T. up on an easel sheet and let the room decide how many and which questions they want to attack. Depending on your team, your time, and your style, you might want to do it our way, or just tell them which questions you're going to ask.

Many of these questions you've likely addressed along the way. It's a market and marketing blueprint. The Brand Action Inventory Task can be applied to your business at any point in time. It is a discipline you should make part of your ongoing brand diagnostics. It's easy to do and forces you to make precise decisions about brand Strengths and Opportunities. Here are some pointers about how it works:

### 1. What's for sale?

This question is about the brand and the product line—positioning and offering.

### 2. Who is the target bull's-eye?

This is an analysis of the ideal customer. Not every consumer, but the ideal consumer behind whom others will follow and fall in line. Demographics. Psychographics. Specifics.

### 3. What is your differentiated benefit?

This isn't just any benefit; it's the single-minded consumer proposition that makes your brand compelling and unique.

## 4. How and when will you make your sale?

This is the brand communications question—media, promotion, Web, direct, PR, etc.—and includes seasonality, geography, and budget decisions.

## 5. What is the messaging?

Yes, this is the Big Idea, the single-minded message and takeaway that will be memorable and motivating to your customer.

## 6. What behavior do you expect?

What do you want the prospect to do—change a point of view, buy your product immediately, or what? This is an important question because most strategies take the result for granted rather than expressing clearly what you want it to be.

## 7. How will you build a brand relationship?

What is going to be the staying power of the message, the ongoing bundle of satisfactions that will bring your customer back for more, to choose your brand over and above another? Oh, yeah, customer repeat—the loyalty idea!

### Marketing Plan in Action

At an industry conference, we asked people to volunteer their answers to the question "What's for sale?" One by one, we pointed out that the answers were identical—and if they couldn't make a distinction between themselves and their competitors in the room, how could their customers possibly make the distinction? As they started to understand the need to differentiate, the attendees started to look—sometimes for the first time in their careers—at what made them different or better than their peers.

Where will this lead you? The sky's the limit. If you answer these questions well, you might be able to take your company and your brand in a direction that seems incredibly obvious but wasn't apparent before the session. Like UPS. How many people know today that the brand was United Parcel Service? How many people even know what a parcel is? UPS. They used their nondescript color brown and created a piece of branding out of it with a great line: "What Can Brown Do for You?" They train or retrain all their delivery people to be virtual best friends with the people to whom they deliver.

But the kicker here for our purposes is what UPS did to extend from just delivery to mailing. Makes sense that a company that delivers stuff should give customers the opportunity to mail stuff, too. So what to do? Open stores, right? Well, maybe. But in the case of UPS, their path to this new market was an acquisition. By buying Mail Boxes Etc., an innovative private packaging and mailing location, UPS became a player in the mailing business, elegantly and instantly.

In March 2001, Mail Boxes Etc.'s parent company was in bankruptcy. UPS was able to pick up their forty-three hundred stores for less than $200 million—about $46,000 a store! An easy rebranding exercise and today the world has ready access to UPS Stores. Brand integration. A very efficient path to market where someone had already built out the business UPS could add to its product and service lineup. Three years later, FedEx countered by acquiring twelve hundred Kinko's stores . . . and as of 2008 they were still rebranding the locations as FedEx Business and spending a lot more than $46,000 a store.

You've got to complete your B.A.I.T. analysis fairly regularly in order to keep your business model current. Your audience will be constantly shifting its tastes and its preferences. You've got to stay on top of those changes and be prepared to move your marketing and brand strategies in the right direction. But this is why they hired you. And if you do it well, this is where you're gonna end up making the big bucks.

So go for it!

# 26

# Open Your Toolbox

"We shall neither fail nor falter; we shall not weaken or tire . . . give us the tools and we will finish the job."

—WINSTON CHURCHILL

TELEVISION IS NO LONGER THE SINGLE, DOMINANT FORM OF ENtertainment in America. Americans under the age of thirty spend more time on their phones and online than they do watching TV or listening to radio. You've got to dip into a vast toolbox of new marketing vehicles to reach consumers in their active lifestyles, as opposed to the media with which you're most comfortable.

The marketing toolbox has never been so varied. In fact, one of our partners refers to it as a toy box, not toolbox, because of the range of fun choices he now has available to him. Once upon a time, marketing was pretty much bound by the simplicity of what we now call TRaP—Television, Radio, and Print. Going to market was a costly proposition and the impediment to market was often the enterprise of the big boys: major marketers with deep pockets.

Today, in the digital age, any Tom, Dick, or Harry (or Bill, Steve, or Sergey) can put a digital shingle out there and be in business. Pretty exciting. And if the buzz of your branded content, Web site, YouTube video, blog, or Twitter following catches enough of a cool breeze, you might not only be in business, you may be in the money on your way to a megahit brand.

So what's the toolbox? It's every way, any way, and the integrated way you go to market. What tools will you use to reach your customers, to deliver your product or service, to drive your customer relationship management (CRM)? The tools are changing and expanding every day. Here's a glimpse of what you can reach for today:

**MEDIUM**

Print
Radio
Direct mail
Outdoor
Television
Point of purchase
Promotion
Direct response
Infomercials
Podcasting
Vcasting
Blogs
Mobile messaging
Interactive kiosks
New out-of-home

Electronic signage
Community sites
Social networking
Banner ads
Product placement
Affinity marketing
Branded content
Video sites
Webisodes
Meta tags
AdWords
Buzz marketing
Guerrilla marketing
Advergaming
Virtual Words
Microblogging

Can you do them all? As Paul likes to say, "Just because you can doesn't mean you should." As of this writing, advertisers are rushing off to get involved with blogging and community sites. At the same time, we're seeing blog burnout and community site constipation: More and more young people are less and less interested in having three thousand "friends" in multiple places clogging their lives with meaningless trivia.

So what do you do if you haven't got the money or means to be in all those media? In fact, no one does—not even the deepest pocket megamarketers. Let your Big Idea dictate the points of engagement. The medium and its method are always in the service of the message—the idea. It has to be simple, elegant, and compelling. The media will follow. Once you know what you want to say and to whom you want to say it, then where you say it will become much more obvious.

## CHOOSING THE TOOLS (WORKOUT)

What are you looking to achieve over the next year for your business? How are you going to achieve it? If you've got a large group, have them work in teams of five or six. If you've got eight or fewer people in the session, have them work together or split into two groups. The assignment is to take your Big Idea and figure out which communication platforms are going to be most effective in putting it across. How would it execute on these different platforms? So if your Big Idea is "Just Do It," maybe you want a Web site where people can put up their own videos of themselves "just doing it." The objective here is to get people thinking of the different ways your Big Idea can get in front of your customers to attract attention and garner stickiness and buzz. Don't worry about your budget right now. What you're trying to establish is where the best place is to put your message. Remember, the idea is the driver—message leads and trumps media.

If you've got two or more teams doing this exercise, have each group present its ideas to the room. Then have a discussion period where people contribute to and refine the various ideas. If time permits, once you've got a list of good ideas, you should vote. Give everyone stickies and have them pick their favorite five or eight or ten ideas from the list. Voilà! You've now got a prioritized list of communication platforms. See chapter 29 (The Money Thing) to understand how to further evaluate and prioritize this list and turn it into the Plan.

## Marketing Plan in Action

We went through exactly this exercise with a packaged-goods marketer who called us for an assignment that was budget-driven. The challenge was to "come up with a Big Idea for a set budget or the CMO is going to redeploy the budget to another brand." How many of you have heard that before? The assignment was clear. In the MPD session we landed on an idea and then went about opening the toolbox to find its optimal translation for the budget allocation. We explored a wide range of solutions, many of them digital because we could more fully realize the idea in a cross-platform campaign within the limited budget. We identified trade-offs in tools—to get to a budget range—without compromising the integrity of the proposed Plan to deliver the idea.

This explosion of media alternatives is the hottest and most fun, most challenging, and most painful issue facing marketers today. Everyone is afraid to give up their traditional media buy: Television, Radio, and Print. That's why we call it a "TRaP." Marketers have fallen into the trap of being committed to old media choices that aren't pulling their weight. And in a tough economy or challenging budget situation, the premium on making smart decisions regarding communication platforms becomes that much more important. It's a creative art and a creative act.

We're all often guilty about going with the tried and true. Part of it is your agency's fault. Agency compensation hasn't caught up with new media. In general, agencies don't get paid nearly as well for a digital solution as they do for a traditional media buy. If they don't make a commission on a blog, why tell the client they have to have one? As a result, companies are faced with different vendors telling them different information: The ad agency, media buying company, and digital media company all have different agendas—and different compensation schemes. So who's really looking out for the brand's best interests? And with a fixed (or decreased) budget, companies are reluctant to move away from traditional media to platforms that can't be measured.

Hint: Do what Coca-Cola and other global marketers are doing—unify your media planning and digital platforms under one department. Make sure your traditional media people get training in the new media alternatives and make sure your new digital people understand traditional media planning. Then integrate the whole unit and start reconnecting with the customers you've been losing for the past five years. Break down the silos and integrate your thinking and your operation.

Our toolbox is an interim step for you. By the time this book is published, it will be out-of-date in terms of tools. There will be new toys and tools for you to place in your consideration set. Bravo. And while the rest of this book is evergreen—you could have used it ten years ago or ten years from now—that toolbox page will feel so five minutes ago each time you confront a new toolbox opportunity. So add your own tools to the list. Keep it up-to-date, make sure your marketing team knows what each tool is for and does well, and keep reaching out across the entire digital landscape.

# 27

# Dream Team

"Coming together is a beginning. Keeping together is
progress. Working together is success."

—HENRY FORD

WHETHER YOU'RE AN ENTREPRENEUR WITH A START-UP OR A
middle or senior manager in a major company, who's coming to the
table to help you achieve your vision?

This is your dream team.

It might be everyone you've assembled for your MPD. If so,
congratulations! You did an extraordinary job on your guest list in
identifying the key players you'll need in the coming months. But
chances are there are people, departments, and companies that
aren't in your session but need to be part of your executional plan.

If you're a siloed Fortune 500 company, it might involve another
department. If you're a growing business of one hundred or more,
it might involve four or five key people outside your department.
You might want to bring in some of your key vendors. Are you a
start-up dot-com company? If so, your dream team may involve
your brother-in-law the lawyer, or your accountant, who will help

with finance and financing. It can include your wife, who shared in your vision all along. The key is to surround yourself with believers and with talent: players who will help you advance your brand proposition.

### Marketing Plan in Action

The principals of a start-up had members of four outside companies participating in their Marketing Plan in a Day. They could see firsthand, hour by hour, the contribution that some of the people were making to the strategic goals of their company. By the time the session was over, the president and chief marketing officer already knew they were going to ask one of the attendees to assume a position on their board, and they have been meeting regularly with one of the other attendees as a possible funding partner. It was a win-win for both the investment banker who volunteered to come and the start-up that added critical talent to the team.

## ACTION TEAM

In the case of our preceding example, the CEO of the start-up wanted a player who was happily ensconced in a major media company. Conventional wisdom had it that this guy wouldn't possibly be available or interested in joining the start-up. But the lure of the idea and the thrill of making it happen brought the player on board in a risk-reward scenario from which there's been no looking back. We're seeing more and more of that today: big players in major companies who are more than willing to jump for the entrepreneurial Opportunity to build something from an early stage for the possible big rewards of equity in a new winner.

So make sure your dream team comprises players you keenly want to play with. You want them to be people and organizations who are going to advance your objectives every day in ways that are original, progressive, and not duplicative of what you do. If your vision is big and smart enough, everyone is fair game. And the best and brightest will want to join you on your adventure.

Selecting the dream team is often easier in a start-up or entrepreneurial venture because you can recruit all the players you want. In bigger, more established organizations, you often have to do business with the players already on the roster. Make sure they pull their weight or replace them. Harsh? Perhaps. But in this global, digital, competitive landscape, you really can't afford to work with anyone but the best.

## YOUR DREAM TEAM (WORKOUT)

A new ad agency? A digital media team? A new product group? The head of sales? Whom do you really want and need on your action team? This can get a bit sensitive if there are people in the room you don't want on the team (unless they are some of those value-added players who don't expect an ongoing role). Make it a bit easier on yourself: Start by identifying team roles. As in sports, everyone plays a specific position. Each player offers a specific area of expertise that contributes to the team chemistry. It's no different here. What key roles do you need to fill in your organization? Then, who best to fill them—both in-house and in partnership or vendor relationships. Identify the team in terms of real players as well as roles needed but perhaps not yet identified or in place. One simple way to start is to ask who wants to take responsibility for what. You'll often be surprised how the tech programmers suddenly will want a role in the actual marketing/branding of the company. Or how a traditional media person will want to explore the new media.

Identifying the dream team is a powerful endorsement of the will to succeed. If you can name the key roles and players and are confident that each one can carry the ball, then you're on a path to success as the team that will pull its weight in achieving the brand mission.

# 28

# Who Ya Gonna Call?

"First, make yourself a reputation for being a creative
   genius.
Second, surround yourself with partners who are
   better than you are.
Third, leave them to get on with it."

—DAVID OGILVY

IN THE PREVIOUS CHAPTER WE TALKED ABOUT A DREAM TEAM OF
people and companies you work with or who report to you. The
other members are outside partners. What company or external re-
source can add value to your brand proposition? How can you extend your brand with someone else's talent, brand, distribution, or
some other contribution to your efforts at little or no cost to you?

Think strategic alliances and prospective partners. Who can
market with you and get positive results from the relationship?
Who should be marketing with you? Who has a business, brand, or
business platform that is complementary to yours and that can add
firepower to your offering? A term we've recently heard is "cooperti-
tion." Competitors you can cooperate with. We talked about UPS

and Mail Boxes Etc. and FedEx/Kinko's in chapter 25 (Follow the Yellow Brick Road). From the customer's point of view, those are matches made in convenience heaven. You don't have to look for a company to buy (or one to buy you), but you can be thinking about strategic alliances that can make dollars and sense. Selling peanut butter? Why not team up with a jelly maker for a special recipe promotion. Got milk? Well, then, Oreos are definitely "milk's best friend." The possibilities are limitless—and your budgets aren't. So think promotion and partnership!

A dream partner promotion that comes to mind is one we tend to see every spring. We're getting into the summer mood, spring-cleaning, thinking outdoor activities and barbecues. Along comes the freestanding insert with the backyard barbecue promotion. A bunch of brands from a bunch of different companies that can fulfill our barbecue dreams. Charcoal, paper cups and plates, ketchup, mustard, relish, hamburger and hot dog rolls, and more. All on display in the ad, all with coupons that give us an incentive to act now. It puts complementary brands in the context of the event. Next time you go to the store, the insert likely goes with you. You stock up and save on a bunch of products you might not have purchased together or at that time and you've saved on every item. It's a win-win for all players.

### Marketing Plan in Action

Wichita, Kansas, is home to four major airplane manufacturers: Cessna, Beechcraft, Learjet, and Mooney. At a workshop last year at one of the companies, we developed a list of marketing Opportunities for their current and future propeller and jet aircraft. One of

> the ideas they came up with was a "Wichita Fly-In." Since there was already a civic "Wichita Days" initiative, the idea came up about sponsoring a multimanufacturer weeklong gathering similar to the Oshkosh Fly-In. It would be a coopertition initiative involving all four companies—and could be win-win-win-win.

When you think about alliances, don't restrict yourself to the packaged-goods category. Discovery Channel and History Channel regularly produce television specials tied into the release of a major motion picture. The movie studio gets the additional publicity and promotion on the cable network and the networks get the additional publicity and promotion of an "advanced screening" of a summer blockbuster hit. Much of the licensing business is based on product that is sold as a result of the excitement surrounding entertainment events. The product placement business, similarly, is all about featuring products in usage contexts that make them more appealing and desirable. Let your imagination take flight—which is the point of the Workouts for this section:

## DREAM PARTNER (WORKOUT)

What's the one company you'd most like to do business with (and why)? What are their core values, features, and customer service capabilities that most appeal to you? How could you adopt them for your company or find a capability that adds that to yours? Most important, what's in it for both companies? What can they lend to your marketing program that has benefit for them . . . and for you?

## PRACTICAL PARTNERS (WORKOUT)

Will Tiger Woods agree to be your spokesperson? Could you afford him? If not, it's time to take your Dream Partner list and refine it with the addition of partners with whom you could realistically hope to pair up. Again, either as a group or in teams, think about all the possible partners for your upcoming campaign or possible promotions. When everyone has thought of their best ideas, have a voting session to determine which ideas have the most "heat" in the room. Which companies make the most sense to do business with? Why? What's the win-win for your company and theirs, and what's the outreach that's going to give you the best chance of cutting a great deal?

What brands make the most sense to share your brand "space"? What are some good ideas that will entice them to give you a big yes? It's a big Opportunity to hitchhike on another's brand karma and associate your brand with the positives that attract customers to them . . . and you. These brands are your friends. They could become important and profitable partners.

Doing business with like-minded companies offers multiple benefits. There's great learning to share. There are new Opportunities to be cultivated all the time. There's the potential for new marketing Opportunities that don't yet exist.

A great example is the world of Apple Computers . . . er, Apple Inc. Apple has endured and thrived through many company iterations, product innovations, and partner initiatives. In the early days of Apple, their computer business was about ease of use and beautiful design. No partners, no collaborators. The PC world and big bad

Microsoft were viewed as the evil empire. By not doing business with these players, Apple came to the brink. Reluctant deals with Microsoft, among other initiatives, virtually saved the computer company.

In the next paradigm breakthrough for Apple, the iPod (once again, a closed system) was its strength and its risk. The iPod/iTunes system has prevailed to render iPod the leading MP3 system in the marketplace by a wide margin. Each one made the other a huge success. Apple saw the Opportunity to rescue a music business that was on its knees and lock up a business model that made sense for everyone. But now everyone's gunning for iPod.

Third time's the charm. The iPhone is the latest paradigm buster for Apple. It's loved, it's elegant, it's state-of-the-art, *and* it has opened its doors to third-party developers who create applications—a business that barely existed before the iPhone. As competitors look to neutralize Apple's iPhone with elegant interfaces all their own, iPhone's apps store offers more bells and whistles for iPhone than competitors can possibly match. To the victor belong the spoils.

In fact, these apps have now taken on a marketing life all their own. As competitive PDAs (personal digital assistants) have come on the market, the first question the reviewers (and customers) ask is: How many apps are there for this phone? These third-party apps cost Apple nothing, but increase brand desire and loyalty every day. Good friends make good business. A win-win for the apps (and the inventors, who in some cases have made big bucks) and a big win for iPhone.

Of course, finding the ideal partner might take time . . . and money. Back in the days of the VHS/Beta videotape wars, Steve was working for Sony's advertising agency, fighting a losing battle to make their superior product (Betamax) the dominant video format. In a last-ditch effort, we made a presentation at Sony's U.S. headquarters and told them they needed software (videotapes) in stores so that people who bought Betamax machines would have movies to watch.

The Japanese managers listened to us politely and silently and thanked us for our efforts. We never heard another word from them about this issue—until two years later, when Sony bought Columbia Pictures. Talk about solving the software issue! That was one very elegant job of vertical integration.

So start thinking about your business beyond the confines of your current model. Know your enemies and either make them friends—frenemies—or make sure they don't eat your lunch. Or eat you for lunch. Know your friends, explore new prospects, make new friends, and do business with them. Done well, 1+1 = 3.

# 29

# The Money Thing

"You can fool all the people all the time if the
advertising is right and the budget is big enough."

—JOSEPH E. LEVINE

NOW COMES THE REALITY OF FIGURING OUT HOW MUCH IT'S GONNA
cost you to put this together.

Notice how far into the MPD outline budget shows up. If you
start with your budget, you're going to restrict your thinking before
you can even start to have a single good idea. By letting the ideas
and discussion develop first, you now have a new perspective on
what's important—and what should be funded!

The bad news, of course, is that you don't have enough money to
do everything you want to do. The good news is that you're not
alone. We were making a presentation to the marketing group at
Coca-Cola a few years ago and one of their product managers sighed
and said, "There's never enough money to do the job right." On the
other hand, you could take the point of view of our late, great friend
and media guru Gene DeWitt. He was commenting to us about

Microsoft's launch of Windows 98, in which they used the Rolling Stones (among others) to announce their new operating system. "Anyone can launch a new product with $150 million," Gene snorted. "The real art is doing it with $5 million." Or in today's entrepreneurial world, there are plenty of start-ups that are building businesses for a lot less than that.

So what should you do? Well, the really great news is that you already have on the wall a comprehensive list of everything you want to do: You've come up with your Big Idea, you've gone through your toolbox (and ranked your tools by importance for the task), you've come up with partnership promotional ideas (and ranked their importance)—so you know everything you want to spend money on.

## JUST BID IT

The simple solution is to give your various suppliers and partners a detailed list of what you want to do and ask them to bid it. If their total estimate is lower than your planned budget, then you don't have a problem. Just start delivering on the items. But let's say you know, even before you send the Plan out for bids, that what you want to do is going to cost more than you've got. Now you've got to make some choices . . . and this is where you start earning your bucks as a marketing manager. There are three ways to land on a budget:

## BRAND AVAILABLE

This is all about the reality of what you've got to spend. It could be dictated by a CMO. It could be based on the projections of the business relative to the margins you must achieve. But it's a fixed budget that has to do the job.

## SHARE OF CATEGORY

This is a number you plug in based on spending in your category and what it will take to match your projected position in the category with the share of voice that should get you there.

## TASK

This is a budget range that is set based on what you believe it will take to achieve your business objectives. You can look at it on a one-year or multiyear basis. But it is best to look at a dollar range that will pay back because the results you will achieve will build the business to levels that are consistent with success.

In every one of these budget plays, start by putting estimated numbers against your toolbox wish list. Now hold your breath. Total it all up and see where you come out. If you are in budget range for brand available or task, congratulations. More likely, you're over what you have or believe you can spend, in which case it's time for triage. The object here is to make cuts—either in tools or in allocations behind tools—that won't compromise the integration of the Plan idea or the integrity of each of the elements that will run as part of the Plan.

### Marketing Plan in Action

At a recent MPD with a major marketer, the budget portion of the session revealed some serious discontent. The company was locked into long-term sponsorship deals with professional sports organizations. These deals had multiyear time commitments and the company had lost some serious marketing flexibility and agility. Long-term commitments might seem like a great deal at the start; but in this era of rapidly changing consumer touch points, they can often become impediments to managing your marketing budget to best meet your consumers' changing lifestyles.

It's a negotiation and a give-and-take of tough choices. But it's also a dynamic process that will enable consensus to be the taskmaster of achieving the on-budget Plan. The cuts need to be achieved collaboratively, silo-free, to ensure that the resulting choices are achievable, make sense, and are interactive and integrated.

## GAME DAY (WORKOUT)

It's time to take the field. Who—what tools—are you going to put out there to win? You know your team budget is limited. Have the team decide what tools are necessary to enable you to advance the ball down the field. Which ones are nice to have but aren't essential? Then populate the field with the "players" who will support one another to get you across the goal line.

The important thing is to make sure the objective drives the budget, not the other way around. Too often we see marketers start with the spreadsheet before they've started with a Marketing Plan in a

Day. And priorities that really need to be addressed get pushed into future years because they run out of money before they've even committed to thinking of ideas.

Do it this way first. Have the ideas, then go find the money. It's a lot more creative, a lot more fun, and will produce far more effective results.

# 30

# What Does Victory Look Like?

"I think the measure of your success to a certain
extent will be the amount of things written about
you that aren't true."

—CYBILL SHEPHERD

YOU'RE ALMOST READY TO ASSIGN RESPONSIBILITIES, WRAP UP THE
meeting, and roll out your new Marketing Plan. Almost. Because
chances are you haven't determined in advance what success looks
like. It's a really important strategic decision for yourself, your partners, your stakeholders, your bosses, your investors . . . even your
customers. You've got to manage expectations. Set them up front.

## DEFINE SUCCESS (WORKOUT)

Have everyone take an index card and write down their definition of
*success*. What is the one single thing you want the new marketing
campaign to do for your business? Is it increased sales? More leads?
More page views? More stickiness on the Web site? More hard orders?
More retail traffic? And what are the dollar results you expect the

campaign to yield? After everyone has written down their answer, have each person read theirs out loud and write them all down on your easel pad (titled Defining Success). Review the submissions. Make sure everyone is in agreement. Or spend a bit more time prioritizing the parameters of success. Even though you've gone through almost the complete session with everyone in sync and with everyone starting by writing their goals, you'll be surprised at how different their expectations and expressions of success may be. Not everyone will agree on what success looks like, but it's critically important that you pool the good ideas and reach consensus.

Too many times we see companies initiate plans and then hold their breath. What are the criteria for success? Should success be measured in terms of brand awareness? Improved brand attitudes? Increasing brand interest? Sales? Share of market? All of these? The key is to manage expectations. Put the metrics in place to measure the results. And get buy-in that the metrics will be the barometer of success.

### Marketing Plan in Action

In one MPD session we asked participants what they thought their customers thought of them. What would their customers say about their products and services? Most couldn't answer the question except by talking about overall sales. We suggested that there are many ways they could learn about customer satisfaction. We landed on a range of different—and largely inexpensive—research methods that would not only refine their metrics of success but also give them guidance on how to improve their offering.

Remember when you were in middle school and you managed your mother's expectation of your report card? You downgraded key subjects so that when the results came in you always performed better. You remember. You prepared her for the B so that the B+ would look really good. It's no different for your business (or a Fortune 500 business). Manage expectations. Perform well, of course. But set your expectations in a profitable but achievable range across clear, measurable goals. Underpromise, overdeliver!

## READ, ROLL, RE-UP

What does success look like? Once you've achieved the results you've led everyone to believe were reasonable, successful, and scalable, it's time to raise the bar. What does big success feel like? Only you can know. But if the goals you've achieved are on par with your most conservative projections, feel a quiet sense of relief and get back to work. You know that's not good enough!

How does success get measured? What is success worth? How can you recommend the expansion of success? These are all questions you need to identify up front, calibrate clearly, and measure cleanly. You want to win on sure ground. Failure is not a deathblow; it's an honest moment in time that can be revised, reordered, and redirected—if you've set the stage for understanding the parameters of failure as effectively as you've set the goals for success. Not everyone wins the first time out.

One of the issues you want to address as your Marketing Plan moves forward is whether you've got the underlying premise right. If you do, then failures are the result of the message proposition, not the Marketing Plan. P&G is a master of understanding the difference between message failure and marketing failure. P&G, in its great marketing wisdom, has encountered and vanquished a number of failures along the way. Time after time, not content to take failure as a final answer, a number of their brands prevailed big-time to become huge category winners through revision and recalibration.

Pampers introduced the first disposable diaper. Seemed like a brilliant idea. Yet launch after launch failed to get the product going. "Convenient." Nope. "Disposable." Nope. "Less Mess." Nope. Eventually, P&G found the winning message: "Keeps Your Baby Drier." And suddenly they had a hit. Because new moms weren't motivated by benefits for themselves, the winning communication was embracing moms' commitment to doing the best for their babies. And that became the winning value proposition. Once P&G landed on the sweet spot for babies and new moms, they had a hit.

Ditto for Pringles. Pringles was a disaster the first time out and several times after that. Yeah, stackability was a nice idea. But these were potato chips—food! If the product didn't taste any good, the convenience factor was a nonstarter. After many reformulations, great tasting, very convenient, nonoily Pringles became a growing success. Taste was the ante. All the other wonderful P&G innovations were merely icing on the cake.

So before you leave the session, make sure everyone in the room agrees on what "success" will look like. That way, you can all have a yardstick against which to measure your results. And as our partner Jeff Woll always preaches: "You can't manage what you don't measure." If you don't know what you want, how will you know when you get it?

# 31

# Where's the Action?
# (Talk's Cheap)

"Take time to deliberate; but when the time for
action arrives, stop thinking and go in."

—NAPOLEON BONAPARTE

THE PROBLEM WITH PLANNING IS OFTEN THE SAME PROBLEM WITH
meetings. You spend lots of time talking, theorizing, even reaching
agreements. It's great that you've built this wonderful Plan, but
it's worth nothing unless and until you put it into play. You need
to develop a specific action plan, with timing, milestones, and
responsibilities.

Who's going to do what, when, how? How will progress and action be implemented and how will it be measured? The final step of
the Marketing Plan in a Day is to build the action plan. This is a
broad-stroke outline to translate plans into activation. The best way
to do it is to build three columns on your easel pad. Title them Milestones, Timetable, and Responsibility.

## MILESTONES

Milestones are actions and activities that are essential to putting the Plan into play. Ideally you'll prioritize your milestones on the easel pad. But it's not critical that you obsess about the order as you identify the projects. The key is to get all the elements of the action plan captured. You can always go back—and you will—to review priorities of events and set the order or reorder them.

Milestones can and should be any of the key issues you've identified in your MPD that you need to advance to move smartly into the marketplace. They can include such items as:

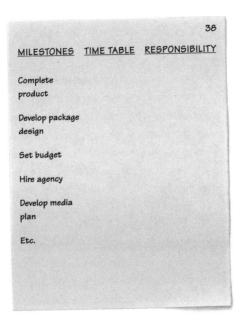

| MILESTONES | TIME TABLE | RESPONSIBILITY |
| --- | --- | --- |
| Complete product | | |
| Develop package design | | |
| Set budget | | |
| Hire agency | | |
| Develop media plan | | |
| Etc. | | |

38

## TIMETABLE

Once you've established your milestones, it's critical that you put dates against them. The dates can be listed as "month of," "week of," or specific dates, depending on the timing needs of your business and Plan. The dates are your test of reasonableness for the milestones. They will help you order and reorder events based on logic and need. Even if you don't know the exact timing of events, establish dates anyway. Take best guesses. Be confident the timings make sense both in meeting business needs as well as in being achievable. This is a critical component of the action plan. Be realistic but be aggressive. The dates are both your guide and your guarantee that you believe in the Plan and are committed to advancing it.

### Marketing Plan in Action

Working with a start-up, a critical question involved what key initiatives they expected to accomplish in their first three years of operation. As a small business, being too ambitious could mean death by indigestion. Setting specific goals and attainable timetables to achieve those goals became a breakthrough for them in the meeting and for their Plan.

## WHO'S RESPONSIBLE?

The third column of the action plan is "Responsibility." Who is the go-to person who will take ownership of the various action items of the Plan? Not a committee, not a group of people. Who is the one person who will take responsibility for moving the action item forward? She can engage as many people as she would like to help. And your organization may have groups or teams already in place to advance initiatives in the various areas you highlight. But when push comes to shove on an item, who are you going to turn to who will ensure that action happens smartly, reliably, and on time?

An up-front review of all the people you need to turn your Plan into action is a good way to ensure that you've invited the right and complete complement of players to your MPD. It's also a great test of affirmation of your action team. This is why we've suggested you read this entire book before you plan the meeting. The meeting—and its resulting Plan—will be way more successful if you've considered simple variables, such as who's going to take charge when you put together your invitation list. If you've gotten your guest list right, it will be easy to fill out your Responsible column. The players will be obvious choices—and volunteers.

## SECTION SIX
# CONGRATULATIONS!

EUREKA! YOU'VE DONE IT! THE DAY WAS EXHAUSTING, BUT, we expect, energizing. You've achieved consensus, you've got a working Plan. It's all up on the walls for everyone to see and feel. So congratulate yourselves. Thank everyone for their time and commitment. Summarize the accomplishment. Let everyone know what the next steps are. Provide a meeting wrap-up, making sure you include a long view of the road ahead. Also make sure everyone knows what comes next, from the write-up of the Plan to its review and implementation. Review your agreements on what testing will be undertaken and what success will look like. And, finally, start thinking about your next Marketing Plan in a Day.

# 32

# Pop the Cork

"A day merely survived is no cause for celebration.
You are not here to fritter away your precious hours
when you have the ability to accomplish so
much . . ."

—OG MANDINO

TAKE A MOMENT TO CONGRATULATE EVERYONE IN THE ROOM!
You've all come together in support of the mission, vision, and idea
that can make your company, business, nonprofit, or dot-com a success. It's been a long, tough—but exhilarating—day, and at the end
of it everyone should feel like there is a clear direction and goal . . .
and a Plan to get there.

You now have a written document everyone can agree on. This is
your marketing blueprint. It's a living Plan that needs to be cared for,
fed, edited, added to, deconstructed, bundled, amended—but most
of all followed. Of course there's still a lot of work to be done—but
the hard stuff is behind you. Possibly for the first time in your organization's/team's/company's/start-up's/nonprofit's history, you've got

an action plan to get everyone focused in the same direction that will engage a dynamic process and produce exciting results.

It's been our experience that people want to embrace the results of the session. They're excited about what they've accomplished and feel like it's the first time everyone in the organization has been truly on the same page. They feel a part of it. They have played an essential role in the shaping of the Plan. They feel ownership of it. They are committed to it and motivated to bring it to life—for the sake and success of the business as well as for their own sakes and success. They are now ambassadors of the Plan and the MPD process.

Don't risk losing that enthusiasm and momentum—but catch your breath. For now, give yourself (and everyone in attendance) a lot of credit. Allow some time for the results of the day to sink in. For openers, take everyone out for a beer. Or soda. Or dinner. Or golf. Extend some shared experience that will let everyone unwind a little bit and share their feelings about what they have accomplished. Or, at the very least, besides the profound thanks at the end of the session, send an e-mail to the team congratulating everyone and summarizing just several of the monumental achievements you accomplished together. Beyond building a workable and working Marketing Plan, the MPD also builds great team spirit and positive momentum. Don't lose the opportunity to reinforce that. So toast your success—and your future as well!

# 33

# Wrap-up/Follow-up

"It ain't over until it's over."

—YOGI BERRA

FOR EVERYONE ELSE, THE MARKETING PLAN IN A DAY IS OVER.
For the facilitator, there's another bit of important work. It starts
with the easel sheets on the wall and the PowerPoint document the
note taker compiled. Those are two key points that we touched on
early in the book and we need to revisit:

1. In chapter 5 (Tools of the Trade) we listed among your tools a
   laptop with PowerPoint and a fast and accurate typist. We hope
   that person carefully and accurately transcribed everything you
   wrote on the walls onto a PowerPoint presentation (that he saved
   frequently). As everyone is gathering up their notepads and empty
   soda cans, look over the PowerPoint slides and make sure you
   understand everything your note taker recorded. Take out a flash
   drive and ask him to put a copy onto your drive right there. Now
   you've got two copies and 80 percent of your additional work is
   done: You've got all the easel notes transcribed.

2. In chapter 12 (In Session) we told you to number each page of the easel pad as you go. Please, please, please, don't treat this step lightly. You're going to have ten, twenty, thirty, or more large easel sheets hanging on your walls, many with different-colored markers and stickies. In the same location on each sheet (top left, top right, bottom right—whatever suits your mood) you've written the number of the sheet. Which is about to make the task of compiling final Plan notes much easier.

Starting with the first sheet, gently peel each one off the wall and stack them together on top of one another, as if you're trying to reassemble the original easel pad. If you do this carefully and well, you'll end up with a stack of sheets numbered consecutively from 1 to the end. Add your Parking Lot slide(s) to the back of the pile. Carefully roll or fold that deck together and take it with you. Now take all that good work, put it in your office or back in your hotel room or someplace safe, and give yourself the evening off! You deserve it!

The next day, while everything's still fresh in your mind, open the PowerPoint notes from the session and carefully, page by page, compare them to the actual easel sheets. *No matter how good your transcriber was, there will be discrepancies.* Accept that. Which is why we urge you to use both during the session. The easel pad and the PowerPoint are a safety check, each one against the other. Mostly you should go with the easel pads . . . because, after all, you wrote them, so you know exactly what you intended. On the other hand, there may have been side comments that you missed while you were writing things down that your note taker caught on the PowerPoint. Use your judgment.

Your task here is not only to make sure you've transcribed the meeting completely and accurately but also to bring clarity to the entire day. You'll want to edit out redundancies and reorder certain points for priority communication or consideration. Additionally, as the moderator—the Leader of the meeting—you know the text and subtext of all of the discussion. So once you've gotten everything transcribed and edited to your complete satisfaction—which will likely take several hours—go back and decide if you want or need to add any moderator commentary. Moderator commentary is elaboration of key points that make the deck clearer and more comprehensive. It's your opportunity to clarify points that may have been key meeting issues. They offer a bridge to content slide by slide, perspective for further reflection, and additional considerations for team follow-up. They also may make the PowerPoint more turnkey—clearer commentary for interested parties who may not have been participants in the MPD.

Your next step is to decide how (and to whom) you want to distribute the final, official PowerPoint Plan. You may decide to send the deck initially to your Planning Partner for review before wider distribution. You may decide that all the people in the meeting receive the deck or just some of them. This is your Marketing Plan blueprint. You want to be sure that the people who receive it are the people who are most fully ready to commit to it and get it implemented.

You may decide to have two versions of the PowerPoint Plan. One is a complete record of the progress of the Plan—the draft you've just edited. The other is a streamlined version of the Plan. It's all the content with less of the process. For example, if you've done three pages of positioning work (e.g., Word Position, Positioning Power Words, Positioning: Round 2), you may decide to just include

Positioning: Round 2 and the final, synthesized positioning boxed or bolded on one slide in the PowerPoint. You can then delete the two previous process slides or move them into an appendix in the Plan that can reveal to management the process that helped you land on your positioning "answer." You get the idea.

Some companies will prefer to have the PowerPoint sent to the CMO or the Planning Partner for review and distribution. Some companies will want the PowerPoint sent to everyone who was in the meeting. It's really a matter of corporate culture. Do whatever makes the most (political) sense within your organization. But the ideal would be a situation where you have permission and agreement to send it to all the stakeholders who participated in the meeting. It provides a living document of your work together and is a final souvenir of your stakeholders working together.

We've worked with companies that prefer the PowerPoint be presented in a follow-up meeting. In that case, the facilitator will be the presenter: You'll review the entire day in a quick one-hour recap. (Don't let this recap turn into a "let's add something" session.) If further work is indicated, next steps should be clearly identified and next actions, meetings, and milestones clearly outlined.

One of the key slides will be the action plan from chapter 31 (Where's the Action? [Talk's Cheap])—who's doing what? Occasionally, some people who were enthusiastic about assignments during the MPD session might find reasons to excuse—or recuse—themselves following the session. It's likely that some ideas developed that hadn't been assigned to someone specific in the MPD session. If that's the case, you've got to make some executive decisions.

If your MPD session was a success, you're going to refocus a lot of team activity and shift toward making your Marketing Plan a reality. We believe that's the job of the senior team members. Or member. That person has to look at who's doing what in the organization and who *should* be assigned to handle key assignments. So make sure the edit of the easel sheets makes the timing, milestones, and responsibilities very clear—and factor that in when you decide to whom to distribute your final PowerPoint or how you need to conduct the follow-up meeting.

Once you've reviewed the easel sheets, accurately written up the PowerPoint presentation, and ensured that the work is turned over for dedicated action, your work as facilitator is officially done.

And in case no one in your organization bothers to say it to you, we will:

Congratulations! Bravo! Well done! You did one hell of a great job! And you're likely feeling richer for the experience and more valuable to your organization both for future MPD work as well as for Plan execution.

# 34

# Road Test!

"... whenever you have been driven to the wall, you have extricated yourself in a way which you never would have dreamed possible had you not been put to the test."

—ORSON WELLES

SHINY CARS IN THE LOT MAY LOOK GREAT. TIRE KICKING IS FUN. As is sitting in the front and back seats. But the real questions are: How does it handle? Take turns? Idle? Accelerate? Brake? How's the visibility? How do all those amenities work on the road?

The same disciplines hold true for your business. Once all the elements are in place, you should take the Plan out for a spin. There are lots of ways to road test your MPD. And we've come a long way from one- and two-year test markets. So this is not about testing forever or analysis paralysis. This is about making sure all the moving parts work well before committing big bucks—or small bucks that feel like big bucks—to putting your Plan and business on the national roadways.

Road testing your Plan can involve any number of ingredients.

Do test runs of your product. Make sure quality control is perfect. Be confident of your pricing. Your suppliers. Your distribution. Run a market test. The good news is that the planning process has identified all the moving parts of the Plan. You know what to evaluate. Now measure the results. Once you're confident all your moving parts are in place and running smoothly, you're ready to launch. All this holds true whether yours is a new product launch, a year-two rollout, a new promotion, or a new initiative for your thirty-year-old brand.

The road test demonstrates whether your Plan is viable. Did you plan a new retail experience or CSR (customer service representative) experience in your MPD? Well, who's going to train your sales reps? Will they be able to translate your good ideas into action that produces results? Did you get all the elements in place to have an impressive business offering? Did you make note of all the winning consumer touch points? Then be sure you earn your trust every day. How are you going to make your rollout feel like a shiny new car every day? If you want your customers coming back for more, you've got to "invite them in" every day.

If you find you need to have a short (two-hour or half-day) MPD for your rollout or test phases, here are a couple of additional exercises:

## DRESSED FOR SUCCESS (WARM-UP)

What's the most impressive store opening you've ever witnessed? We've all seen them. The new corner deli, supermarket, restaurant, or car wash? Beyond the hanging banner that screams, "Hi, we're new, c'mon in," what were all the elements they put in place to impress you that this was a great store, complete in its offering and inviting to you, the consumer? How long did its "newness" last?

## WINNING MIX (WORKOUT)

What are the key elements to a winning mix for your business? If you're a store, we've identified some of the keys to a winning formula. If you're an online business, be sure to carefully evaluate product, navigation, price, and checkout to be sure you're focusing on some of the key winning ingredients.

How many times have we seen the new retail establishment dazzle in its launch and woefully disappoint after its first six months? What's that about (besides an invitation to failure)? It seems to be a constant in the supermarket business. The new store opens with the freshest produce, the most impressive deli counter, the cleanest aisles, and rapid checkout. But it doesn't take long before the produce looks disgusting, the deli salads look days old, the store is filthy, and checkout takes forever. That's it for you and that store . . . you are so on to the next store opening.

Does your strategy hold up? Your positioning? Your mission statement? Your objectives and goals? If you're a major corporation, you probably have research and support groups in place that can do some quick qualitative and quantitative analyses. If you're a start-up or a small business, your "research" might involve asking friends, family, and target prospects what they think of your strategy. It's not nearly as good as real research, but it can give you some serious feedback on whether you're on the right track. Time and again we've seen company owners come back with great relief after they've done this. They see the light go on in people's eyes and it tells them that their message and consumer experience are a match and are right on target.

So do some research. Do some testing. Make sure your aim is true.

Six Months Later . . .

# 35

# How Did You Do?

"Why did you do that? Who knows why anybody
    does anything?"

—MASON COOLEY

AS THE SUN SETS SLOWLY OVER YOUR VERANDA IN TAHITI . . . OH,
but we digress. Unless, of course, you were indeed that successful in
that short a time and moving to Tahiti was your goal.

The Marketing Plan in a Day is a living, breathing exercise that
has to be repeated over and over. Thinking "we've got it solved" will
lead only to the complacency that will make you next year's also-
ran. Today's solution is tomorrow's new challenge. The market keeps
moving. New competitors and new competitive programs are gunning for you. Last year's initiatives are just that: last year's. And the
better they are, the more likely someone will be coming after them,
and you.

New people come on board. CEOs retire. CMOs are hired and
fired. Situations change. Needs change. New marketing opportunities arise. That's what you're really being paid for: to be aware of new

situations and new opportunities and be ready to take advantage of them.

### Marketing Plan (Not) in Action

Confession: For the first six months of our PS Insights business, we didn't do a Marketing Plan in a Day for ourselves. We carried on as folklore. "We know what we're about and what we're doing." We could tell it to anyone. Shame on us. We never wrote it down. We didn't practice what we've been preaching throughout this book. The cobbler's children have no shoes. We finally got around to doing one when our media partner said, "I may have a contact for you—where's your presentation?" Ouch.

The real point of the story is that we ended up doing three separate MPD sessions in the next thirty days. The first one for the benefit of our media partner, our staff—and, of course, us. The second with a half dozen CEOs and senior consultants. The third with just the partners of the business. Each MPD session gave us a different piece of our puzzle, addressing different aspects of our business. But by the time we were done, we had a solid blueprint that could take us forward for the next year.

We try not to go any further than that. Yes, we have three-year and five-year goals for our company (addressed in our Plan), but we recognize that you've got to get there by aiming for specific milestones along the way—accessible, attainable, specific goals to achieve. And our MPD does that for us, for our clients, and, after reading this book, for you. Every time.

So what about you? Did you achieve your goals this year? If not, why not? What are your goals for next year? How are you going to put them on plan to best achieve them? You guessed it. It's time for a Marketing Plan in a Day.

Don't fall into the classic trap of rewriting last year's Plan for next year. Start with a blank sheet of paper and start the process all over again. It won't give you more work, but we will make a guarantee—and it's the only one we're absolutely certain of: It will guarantee you more inspiration, less perspiration, and more productivity toward a common goal.

And by the way, in case you haven't figured it out by now (and we know you have, because you're smart—the fact that you bought this book and read it all the way through is proof of that), the Marketing Plan in a Day will work for you in just about every aspect of your business and your life.

Need a Sales Plan in a Day? Use the same process and you'll get your results.

Need a Business Plan in a Day? Well, as marketers, we don't see much of a difference between a Marketing Plan and a Business Plan, but that's our prejudice. The same process will get you the results you need.

Need a Plan to Get a Better Job? The MPD is ideal. After all, what's job hunting other than the process of marketing yourself?

Need a Plan to Get Your Kids into College? Again, what's a college application other than the process of marketing your kid's high school record?

We honestly believe (and have used) the Marketing Plan in a Day for all those reasons . . . and more. We're sure you're already thinking of different ways you can use it for your own life, job, and career.

Enjoy, good luck, and keep at it!

## SECTION SEVEN
# HIGHWAYS AND BYWAYS

CALL THESE FINAL THREE CHAPTERS APPENDIXES IF YOU like. We've added them to help focus your thinking and your outline for your Marketing Plan in a Day. The Sample Outlines, Sample Timelines, and Sample Warm-ups and Workouts should go a long way to helping you add some creative juice to your sessions!

# 36

# Sample Outlines

"Organization . . . brings specialists . . . into a
working relationship with other specialists for a
complete and useful result."

—**JOHN KENNETH GALBRAITH**

WE TRUST YOU'VE BEEN MAKING NOTES ALL ALONG. GREAT! YOU'VE
likely got lots of great thoughts about the elements that will become
your own meeting outline. But let's take a moment and review what
we talked about in the past hundred or so pages: The "outline" we
described looks like this:

    **i.** Introduction
    **ii.** Parking Lot
    **iii.** Meeting Objective

## 1. Where Are We Now?

        **a.** Business Story
            **i.** Group Storytelling Workout

        **ii.** SWTO Strengths Workout

        **iii.** Power Words Workout

    **b.** Opportunity

        **i.** Capital Investment

        **ii.** Manufacturing

        **iii.** Distribution and Sales

        **iv.** Partners

        **v.** Timing and Milestones

    **c.** Brand Horizons

        **i.** Brand Yes Warm-up

        **ii.** Great Extensions Workout

        **iii.** Simply the Best Workout

        **iv.** Word Position Workout

    **d.** Brand Limits

        **i.** Brand Capabilities

        **ii.** Brand Boundaries

        **iii.** Barriers to Entry

        **iv.** Corporate Agility

        **v.** The Worst Warm-up

        **vi.** Your Worst Workout

        **vii.** The 180 Workout

        **viii.** Attribute/Benefit Workout

### 3. How Will We Get There?

    **a.** The Big Idea

        **i.** Hidden in Plain Sight Workout

        **ii.** Power Words Workout

    **b.** Paths to Market

Ouch! We're exhausted just reading that list. And you'd be foolish and naïve to think you could accomplish all that in a day. But believe it or not, that entire list could be managed in an extensive off-site two-day session.

As a rule of thumb, Paul believes you should allow approximately a half hour for each major letter/outline item. So the above outline would take about ten to twelve hours without breaks. Add introductions, breaks, and meals, and you're looking at fourteen to sixteen hours: two full days.

Not unreasonable. In fact, you could trim out the Workouts and Vision-Mission-Positioning duplication and you'd have yourself a very leisurely two-day session with lots of time for tennis, golf, and group activities:

   i. Parking Lot
  ii. Introduction
 iii. Meeting Objective

## 1. Where Are We Now?

     a. Business Story
     b. Business Objective
     c. Positioning
     d. Competition
     e. Product Line

## 2. Where Are We Going?

     a. SWTO
     b. Opportunity

     c. Brand Horizons

     d. Brand Limits

### 3. How Will We Get There?

     a. The Big Idea

     b. Paths to Market

        i. B.A.I.T.

     c. Toolbox

     d. Dream Team

     e. Action Team

     f. Partners

     g. Budgets

     h. What Does Victory Look Like?

     i. Assign Responsibilities and Timings

### 4. Congratulations/Wrap-up!

This "shortened" outline is nine hours without breaks. A five-hour day and a four-hour day? Fine by us. But many companies just can't spare the time. Which brings us back to what we said in our Meeting Road Map chapter (chapter 6): As you build your own customized outline, you have to decide what's most mission/MPD critical for your team.

1. Where are you now?
2. Where are you going?
3. How will you get there?

Do you know enough about where you are that you can concentrate on where you're going? Do you know where you're going but need to concentrate on how to get there? For openers, think about what the most important section(s) will be for your session. What are the major areas you need to focus on? Then ask yourself where you have to drill down.

Keep in mind what we've been saying all along: As long as you cover the three basic points, a Marketing Plan in a Day is practically foolproof. Ironically, it almost doesn't matter what specific elements populate your outline. What matters is that you answer those three questions really well and truly customize your meeting outline for your MPD business needs. If you get the right questions answered in the right order, you'll build out a meaningful, usable action plan that your entire team can rally around. And to do that, you need topics that advance the conversation.

It's in those topics—points you have to bring out based on your specific issues—that you'll build out a program that works specifically and well for your company. The key is not only in the logic of the Plan but in the emphasis you put on the elements you most need for in-depth discussion and action consensus.

What are those topics? Just about anything you think you need. Review our examples and then use them as a guide—not a format!—to build your own customized Marketing Plan in a Day. But to help you start to shape your Plan, let's take a look at four different outlines that different organizations put together for their own MPD:

# OUTLINE (CASE) STUDY #1

**Marketing Plan in a Day for a Two-Day,
In-depth Brand Repositioning**

DAY ONE

## 1. Where Are We Now?

- **a.** Business Idea
- **b.** Business Objective
- **c.** Vision
- **d.** Mission
- **e.** (Brand) Positioning

*Break*

- **f.** Competition
- **g.** Product Line

## 2. Where Are We Going?

- **a.** Situation Analysis/SWTO

*Lunch*

- **b.** Mining Opportunity
- **c.** (Brand) Horizons
    - **i.** Capabilities

ii. Brand Elasticity

d. (Brand) Limitations

## DAY TWO

### 3. How Are We Going to Get There?

a. Budget

b. Paths to Market

### Break

c. What's the Big Idea?

### Lunch

d. Communication Tools

e. Dream Team

f. Strategic Partners

g. Key Milestones

h. Measuring Success

i. Capitalizing on Success

That was a ten-hour, two-day session for a consumer packaged-goods company that needed to reshape a tired brand. The first day was six hours including lunch. Day two was four hours. That's the closest we're willing to come to a cookie-cutter, in-depth, cross-every-t-dot-every-i outline. We needed two full days for that one because this was a major rebranding. A lot of issues needed to be discussed in-depth. In that session, there was a premium on landing on the creative idea. It provided tremendous action efficiency coming out of the meeting. But it also required a commitment of two days of meeting. Most Marketing Plans in a Day don't need to be that complex. In fact, the simpler and easier the better—for you, for your team, and for the final Plan deliverable.

## OUTLINE (CASE) STUDY #2

### Marketing Plan in a Day for a New Company

The company was less than six months old and growing faster than they originally planned (we should all have that problem). While the growth was happening within the parameters of their business plan, they knew they needed to ramp up their staffing and sales strategies, but didn't want to make the mistake of hiring the wrong people at the wrong price points. They invited some participants who were thinking about investing in the company, so introductions were an important part of the session:

### SESSION OUTLINE

  **i.** Introduction
  **ii.** Meeting objective

**1. *Where Are We Now?***

  **a.** Business Objective
  **b.** Stated Core Capabilities

      **i.** Creative Development

      **ii.** Production

   **c.** Unique Capabilities

   **d.** Current Brand Position

   **e.** Who Are We?

   **f.** What Business Are We In? (One Idea)

## 2. Where Are We Going?

   **a.** Best Business Prospects

   **b.** Categories

   **c.** Customers

   **d.** Relationships

   **e.** Financial Goals and Sources of Revenue

      **i.** 2008

      **ii.** 2009

      **iii.** 2010

## Break

## 3. How Will We Get There?

   **a.** Team/Players

      **i.** Full-time Staff

      **ii.** Part-time Players

      **iii.** Other Players

   **b.** Credentials and Selling

   **c.** Selling Presentation

   **d.** Collateral Materials

   **e.** Web Site and Work Examples

**f.** Plan and Priorities

**g.** Drive Relationships

**h.** Timing and Milestones

**i.** Immediate Needs

Notice that we didn't slavishly follow the names of the key points—because their needs were slightly different. Instead of an in-depth toolbox, we knew they had to focus on a simple group of selling materials: sales force, collateral, and Web. So we didn't waste time delving into new media alternatives. Also, because the partners in the business were sensitive to the word *partners* (they already had enough of those!), we used the phrase "drive relationships" to clarify that we were interested in finding other companies to work with. Most important, they wanted to get at personnel needs. To do that, they needed to agree on where they were and where they were going. That's why the entire "How Will We Get There?" section started with a discussion of who would help them do that. Because they knew what their goals were, they were able to assess people with an eye toward future growth.

Total time? Under five hours.

## OUTLINE (CASE) STUDY #3

### Marketing Plan in a Day for an Organization Looking for Sponsors

This was a straightforward meeting to pull the team together on organization sponsorship. There was no need for introductions—it was an internal team with no participants from other divisions of the organization. They dived right into the issue at hand.

i. Meeting Objective

## 1. Where Are We Now?

a. Unique Capabilities
b. Mission
c. Positioning
d. Review of Sponsorship Lessons Learned

## 2. Where Are We Going?

a. Successes
b. Failures
c. What Is Our Sponsorship Offering
d. Benefits to Sponsors—What's Included?
e. Levels of Sponsorship
f. Prospects
g. Categories and Companies

## 3. How Will We Get There?

a. Selling Presentation
b. Pitch Deck
c. Video
d. Other Collateral Materials
e. Leave-behinds
f. Closing Deals

g. Next Steps and Milestones
h. Pitch Deck Development Schedule
i. Sales Plan Development
j. Scheduled Sales Presentations

The longest part of the entire session was #1b—Mission. While you would think an organization would know their mission, in fact there had been a number of hirings in the previous six months, and there were several people in the meeting who were ambivalent about the stated mission of the organization. Everyone wrote down their mission definition on an index card, but when the leader had them read their answers out loud, there were wildly differing opinions. The greater part of two hours was taken up with a wide-ranging (and occasionally heated) discussion of the mission.

Ultimately, it was the best thing that could have happened. For the first time since they'd been hired, everyone—old hands and new employees—had an opportunity to articulate their idea of the organization's vision. It was something that had been assumed all along (and the assumption was that everyone was in agreement) and the results were electrifying. When everyone finally agreed on the mission, the rest of the session (and the rest of their year) flew by as they all united on what was needed to get sponsorships at all levels.

For that organization, the invaluable part of the meeting was #1: Where Are We Now? If they had assumed that everyone was in agreement, they would have just had a meeting to talk about sponsorship selling materials . . . and it would have led to one meeting after another because everyone involved in the process wasn't on the same page regarding the overall mission. Total time for the session? Four and a half hours.

# OUTLINE (CASE) STUDY #4

## Marketing Plan in a Day to Review Brand Positioning

Here's an example from a successful company that had moved well beyond their founding vision. They were still marketing their company using their launch materials, but who they were in the minds of their customers was very different from their founding vision.

i. Meeting Objective

### 1. Where Are We Now?

    a. Background
    b. Company/Brand Inspiration
    c. History and Highlights
    d. Challenges and Dreams
    e. Mission/Capabilities
    f. Business Concept
    g. Business Goals
    h. Competitive Insulation

### Break

    i. Brand Positioning
    j. Brand Identity (What Do We Stand For?)
    k. Brand Positioning Statement
    l. Product Name(s)
    m. Elevator Speech

*Working Lunch/Break*

### 2. Where Are We Going?

  **a.** Competitive Frame

  **b.** Key Competitors

  **c.** SWTO

  **d.** Competitor Strengths and Weaknesses

  **e.** Current and Near-Term Prospects

  **f.** Needs

*Break*

### 3. How Will We Get There?

  **a.** Driving Momentum

  **b.** Insulating and Extending the Positioning

  **c.** Pitching Key Audiences

  **d.** Pitch Proposition/Deck

  **e.** Driving the Brand

  **f.** Confirming the Business Offering

  **g.** Developing an Action Plan

  **h.** Key Elements of the Plan

  **i.** Implementing the Plan

  **j.** Key Milestones

  **k.** Next Steps

This was a long, difficult session—the entire purpose, mission, sales, and marketing strategy of the company were up for discussion. Obviously, the CEO, CFO, CSO, and CMO were all in the meeting, as were a number of key sales and marketing personnel. It was hardest on the founder/CEO. He'd started the company with a unique vision and it had become something different in the minds of his customers and employees. To his credit, he was willing to dig right in and start all over again if necessary. But at the end of the session, everyone had a handle on what they knew, what they needed to find out, what their customers thought of their brand, and how to reposition the company in the minds of the CEO and key salespeople. Total time? Seven hours including breaks.

We could continue. We could show you twenty or thirty more examples. But your outline needs to be fully customized to your issues and needs. If you think you want to get in touch with us and run your outline by us, you're welcome to do so (Paul@psinsights .com or Steve@psinsights.com). After all, that's what we do. And, as you've probably guessed by now, if you're planning your session in Positano, we will positively respond! But because you've read this book, we think you'll probably be able to do a great outline on your own!

# 37

# Sample Time Lines

"Time is time and money is money.
If you want to save one it's always going to cost you
the other."

—STEVE LANCE

CAN'T GET EVERYONE FOR A WHOLE DAY? BETTER TO TAKE WHAT you can get rather than not assembling the troops at all. Would we love to see every Marketing Plan in a Day run a full seven hours? Absolutely. It will save you hundreds of hours of meetings down the road. But if you haven't got all day, there's still good ground that can be covered in less time:

- 2-Hour Marketing Plan
- 4-Hour Marketing Plan
- Marketing Plan in a Day
- 2-Day Marketing Plan

### 2-Hour Marketing Plan

Two hours is a reasonable amount of time to do one of two things: You can either focus on big-picture strategic issues or drill down into a single Marketing Plan initiative. Big-picture strategic initiatives can include setting marketing objectives; establishing time frames for marketing goals; setting a vision, mission, or positioning. Two hours is not sufficient time to spin out the entire Plan. But accomplishing the big-picture issues can set the stage for the next meeting. A sample outline might include:

✓ Business objective
✓ Vision
✓ Brand capabilities
✓ Brand positioning

Or you can designate a two-hour planning session to take on specific issues in the Plan or to outline specific progress toward implementation of a Plan element. Examples here might include assessing potential strategic partners; appropriating a budget for communication tools; reassessing milestones, timing, and responsibilities. Two hours is a great time frame for confirming and building details into the Plan to ensure smart progress and efficient action.

✓ Budget
✓ Communication priorities
✓ Communication tools
✓ Milestones

✓ Timing
✓ Responsibilities

### 4-Hour Marketing Plan

Four hours provides a good opportunity to do some heavy lifting on key strategic issues of the business. This is a good time frame for a deeper dive into market situational dynamics, a detailed SWTO analysis leading to positioning refinement, or a discussion on key stakeholders to advance the Plan. Here, too, the time frame provides the opportunity to probe in greater detail executional elements of the Plan and how to advance them. A very focused and aggressive four hours can accomplish some variation of the following:

✓ Business objective
✓ Vision
✓ Situation analysis
✓ Competitive frame
✓ Brand capabilities
✓ SWTO analysis
✓ Brand positioning

### Marketing Plan in a Day

This is the recommended form for a complete look at your Marketing Plan for the coming year or a specific period of time. The seven-hour form (with perhaps an extra hour for breaks, lunch, etc.) is sufficient time for you to map the blueprint of your entire Plan for the year. This is the form on which we focused this book and is the most elegant time frame to really tackle your complete marketing challenge in a day. It's the recommended form because it is intensive, collegial, exhausting, and exhilarating. The basic outline covers your variation of the following:

- ✓ Meeting objective
- ✓ Vision
- ✓ Mission
- ✓ Competitive frame
- ✓ SWOT
- ✓ Positioning
- ✓ Budget
- ✓ Paths to market
- ✓ Media selection (toolbox)
- ✓ Strategic partners
- ✓ Milestones
- ✓ Responsibilities
- ✓ Timing/next steps
- ✓ Parking lot

### 2-Day Marketing Plan

The two-day Marketing Plan is a wonderfully elegant form to breathe air into the Marketing Plan in a Day or to add elements of creative brainstorming and ideation to the strategic process. In two days you can do one of two things:

1. A Marketing Plan in a Day broken into two pieces with Opportunities for team-building activities in between. For example, work

one morning, have a golf outing and dinner in the afternoon and evening, and wrap up the next morning. Or start the afternoon of day one, have dinner, and wrap up the morning of day two. Or do a team-building exercise the morning of day one, work on the seven-hour Plan in the afternoon, have dinner, and finish the Plan the next day with more team building in the morning or afternoon. During day two give participants free time in the morning, and a specific assignment (e.g., store checks) to fuel the afternoon session on paths to market, strategic alliances, etc. The combinations are endless.

2. A Marketing Plan in a Day with executional direction and ideation built into a solid two days. This extends the outline from strategic issues into specific executional solutions. It's a great form if you can commit the time. And it's a great time-saver. Imagine not only nailing your mission, vision, positioning, marketing goals, and more but also additionally landing on an insight, an idea, and an executional direction to implement to achieve your marketing objectives. We've done it. It's illuminating, empowering, and very productive.

# 38

# Sample Warm-ups and Workouts

"Work smarter, not harder."

—RON CARSWELL

IN CHAPTER 8 (WARM-UPS AND WORKOUTS) WE DISCUSSED TWO kinds of exercises that can really help in moving your session along. Both are fun. Both are team building. Both really help advance Plan building.

Warm-ups are icebreakers. They get everyone in the mood and mind to tackle brand and business issues without challenging the group to focus on the brand at hand. They're at least one step removed from the strategic issues in the Plan, but they establish a mind-set that will make advancing strategic issues easier, faster, and more productive.

Workouts are exercises that add content and consensus to the Plan. They're "on brand," on agenda, and will "populate" the Plan either as designed or through some voting or other sorting to be included on the easel sheets.

We've highlighted a number of Warm-ups and Workouts through-out the book, but here we include a range of others that can be employed and applied to your plans. There are an infinite number of other exercises you may divine and devise both in the planning of your MPD in outline development or on the spot in the meeting as an inspirational idea to break a logjam or advance thinking in other ways. As you devise new Warm-ups and Workouts, we'd welcome your sharing them with us.

Most of the examples that follow will be designated as Warm-ups because we have no specific brand plan at hand here. But many of them could be repurposed to become Workouts if and as you specify the exercise to your brand plan tasks.

In no particular order, here are a few with some descriptors of how they might play out. Keep in mind that the exercise ideas are endless and that the ways in which you employ and apply them are limited only by your imagination.

## ACTION EXERCISES

These Workouts are literally about exercise. Expand the mind by liberating the body. Have people stand up, jump up, do jumping jacks, yoga, potato races—anything that shakes off the cobwebs and gets people relaxed and ready to move on.

### WOULDA COULDA SHOULDA'S . . . OR IF ONLY'S

You can do these for your brand or someone else's. It's the opportunity to explore the roads not taken: If only the brand had introduced a line extension earlier; if only the brand had signed on with a strategic partner; we shoulda spent more money in year one; we coulda offered a premium with the original purchase; if we woulda set an introductory pricing policy . . . You get the picture. Do it for your brand. Or, if it's less painful, evaluate another business where *woulda, coulda, shoulda's* might have saved the day.

## WORD ASSOCIATION

Word associations are great for lots of marketing work. It's often a home-run exercise for new-product development. If you're in the fragrance business, from bathroom fresheners to fine fragrances, imagine what word stimuli such as *Tahiti, Hawaii, Big Sur,* or *Caribbean* can do to move the crowd to brand aroma, flavor, taste, or other relevant associations.

## FLASH CARDS

Another great idea generator, flash cards of virtually any relevant content can drive great thinking from the crowd. If you're in a winter products business, any visuals from a steaming cup of hot chocolate to a snowball fight, a giant fire in a hearth, or people in a hot tub can stimulate thinking that surrounds the experience of winter fun.

## WHAT DOES AN IDEA LOOK LIKE?

These are drawing exercises. Let people have at it with markers and paper. The artfulness of the idea ideologue doesn't matter a whit. It's what people think the idea should "look like" or "be" that's the driver of this exercise.

## MUSIC

Music is fun, relaxing, and a good vehicle for intros, outros, and breaks. You can plan on having music in the session or an iPod ready to play key songs that might thematically advance discussion. You could also choose specific tracks to stimulate mood or imagination mind springs specific to your task.

## DESERT ISLAND PROPS

These are the classic "If you were stranded on a desert island and could have only three things (or five things, whatever), what would they be?" It's about well-being, entertainment, self-expression. It gets to the fundamentals of survival. What do you need to be sure your business survives, thrives, and flourishes?

## INDISPENSABLE BUSINESS SUPPLY

This was one that Staples used as a desert island question to get an alpha panel of product samplers and connectors. Paul suggested using a Sharpie to be able to write everything down both as a Help message and for journal entries. He's been enjoying the free samples and coupons from being a Staples alpha panel member ever since.

## DESERT ISLAND MUSIC

This one's always fun. What are the three or five artists, records, or songs that would be indispensable if you were stranded on a desert island? Why?

## DUMB—OR NOT SO DUMB—JOKES

Jokes are great icebreakers. Humor makes the group feel comfortable upon arrival (e.g., "Welcome to the Marketing Plan in a Day. For the next seven hours you'll feel as if you've spent a month of your time in marketing prison . . . but really, folks . . .") Or, better, a well-placed joke that extends the value proposition of your brand. To wit: A woman ran across Pablo Picasso at a café. She was so excited to see the master that she asked him if he would give her a souvenir doodle of their meeting. In a few seconds, Picasso dashed off a wonderful piece of line art and handed it to her. The woman, so pleased to have this original Picasso, asked if she could please compensate the master in some way. Without a moment's hesitation, Picasso said, "That will be twenty-five thousand dollars." The woman, shocked, responded, "But it took you only a matter of seconds to create this work." Again, without hesitation, Picasso responded, "No, my dear, it took thirty-five years."

## FAVORITE/INDISPENSABLE WEB SITES

We've referenced this one, but it's becoming one of our favorite icebreakers and we use it a lot because it's so lifestyle- and business-relevant. We ask people to list their three favorite sites besides the usual suspects (Google, Yahoo!, Amazon, Wikipedia, MSN, etc.). It's a great way to get at indispensable content. Where do we go, why do we go there? What information do we always seek out? Almost invariably, people want to know about other people's favorite sites.

## ICEBREAKERS

Social games, Warm-up exercises, introductions . . . any kind of ice-breaker that gets everyone on the same page and offering up the same content. These can include favorite movies, songs, Web sites, where you grew up, favorite country, favorite vacation . . . even an amusing game of telephone.

## HOW'S THE WEATHER?

Always an easy one to get everyone on the same page. People just love to talk about the weather. It's beautiful; it's miserable; it will be better tomorrow. What's the forecast for next weekend? What are the best climates in the world?

## VACATION DESTINATIONS

Favorite vacations put people in a good mood. Where do you like to go? Where have you gone most recently? Where will you be going next? When? And why?

## FAVORITE COUNTRIES

What country most appeals to you? Is it about the people? The sights? The food?

## BIRTH ORDER

Birth order carries with it all kinds of interesting agendas. A discussion of traits people think they have based on birth order can be interesting in general and possibly even used to choose up teams for breakout exercises.

## TRUTH OR DARE . . . TWO TRUTHS AND A LIE . . . TRUST EXERCISES

Trust and truth exercises can be risky: Many people are uncomfortable revealing what they think is their "private" self. But these exercises can also offer a good return. If you dedicate two days to your Marketing Plan, doing team-building work possibly with a team-building expert can streamline quality and consensus in the planning process. Two Truths and a Lie is an old camp game where a person says three things about herself; two of them are true and one is a lie. The group has to figure out which one is the lie. Steve loves playing this one, as he starts with "I was arrested for stealing a car. I was arrested for hijacking an airplane. I was jailed for failing to reveal a source in a newspaper article." Go ahead, guess. This example always makes Paul squeamish about being Steve's business partner.

## BOARD GAMES

What are your favorite board games? Why? What are the game-play dynamics of the board game that translate to marketing? To your marketing?

## VIDEO GAMES

Same as above, but different play dynamics. In our Xbox, Wii, Guitar Hero world, video games are moving from skill and action to all kinds of new play. What are those new paradigms of play? What are some new interactive paradigms for your brand?

## VIRTUAL WORLDS

If you could create a virtual world, what would it be? What's the theme? What goes on in there? What kinds of people populate the world? Why do they "live" there? What marketers advertise there? Why?

## PAINT OR CRAYON COLORS

What are your favorite colors? More than the sixty-four pack of Crayola, what are your favorite paint colors? For what places and spaces, rooms or moods?

## FAVORITES

In any category, ask people to list their favorites. Who are your favorite superheroes? Who are your favorite fictional characters? Why? What are your favorite movies? What did you like most about them? The story line/screenplay? The acting? The cinematography? The directing? The editing? And which of these disciplines are most relevant to your brand marketing? What's your favorite book? Your favorite food? You get the idea.

## MOST EMBARRASSING MOMENTS

They usually are traced to your tween years. (Comedians say that "comedy is tragedy plus time.") And they are usually about something bodily personal. Ripped pants, a booger, a fart. They're funny to offer up and can provide a useful watch-out for not making a fool of yourself in the marketplace.

## BEST LIFE DECISION

Maybe it was marriage, maybe kids, maybe job, maybe a place you lived. What's the best, most important decision you're going to make about your business marketing?

## BEST TEACHER

In the formative years, which teacher inspired you most? Name names. Name age and grade. What was it that made this teacher memorable, motivating, and successful in inspiring you to learn?

## BEST COURSE IN SCHOOL

What was the best course you ever took in school? How old were you? What grade were you in? Why was the course a winner? What did you learn? How has that learning stayed with you? How is it applicable to your marketing task at hand?

## BEST BOSS EVER (OTHER THAN YOUR CURRENT ONE)

This is about the traits of leadership and inspiration. What do we value about mentoring? About positive reinforcement? Support? Promotion? Raises? Career advancement? We want the same for our brands, and that productivity can drive all the good things a great boss can bestow upon you.

## WORST BOSS TRAIT (OTHER THAN YOUR CURRENT ONE)

Kind of fun and certainly cathartic. Don't name names, but ask people to identify their worst boss trait. Then ask them to flip that trait 180 degrees. What happens? Sometimes it can yield some inspiring insight into ways to manage your business.

## KINDEST ACT

Random acts of kindness. What was the kindest thing someone did for you or to you? What's the one standout thing you've done that made you feel really great about yourself? What kinds of specific CRM "acts of kindness" will you offer up to your customers?

## FAVORITE LETTERS . . . FAVORITE WORDS

A literate game that can be fun, and who knows where it will wind up? Why do we like the letters we do? Shape? Our initials? Where they fall in the alphabet? What about words? Do we like them for their sound? Their meaning? Their use or how esoteric they are? *Syzygy* is always a good one.

## DREAM JOB

This is always a fun one. Dream big. Would you like to be president? A famous artist? A sports star? The pope? Why? What would make the job satisfying and how can you translate that kind of satisfaction to your marketing?

## DOODLE . . . OR THE FIVE-LINE DRAWING

A five-second doodle. A drawing using only five lines. Who knows where this will take you? Treat it as an icebreaker Rorschach kind of event. Draw and discuss. What do you see? How can you apply it?

## WASTE-TIME CRIME

In business today the kind of time and amount of time wasted is mortifying. What are the biggest waste-time crimes you can think of? How can they be avoided? What's the takeaway(s) for your team?

## CHRISTMASTIME

Give yourself a budget for Christmas spending (unless you still believe in Santa Claus) and identify everyone you need to buy a gift for. What are you going to buy to satisfy everyone on your list and not overspend your Christmas fund?

## IN GOOD COMPANY

Forget about your business and brand for a minute. Ah, relief. If you could work for any company or on any brand in the world, what would it be? Why? What do you respect about them? What turns you on about them? Is it the product or the service? Is it their company culture? Their marketing? Sales?

## FIXER-UPPERS

Think of something that appeals to you that needs major attention to make it viable—a house, a park, an abandoned movie theater. What do you need to fix it up? What would be the best tools to accomplish the task? How can you accomplish it most effectively?

## ROTISSERIE

It's certainly easier to select dream teams for sports than for your own business. So as a Warm-up, you may want to do just that. Work collaboratively or go around the room and select starters for the team of your choice. Basketball, football, and baseball are natural subjects, but your team exercise could be forming a supergroup rock band or a ballet company, or casting or recasting for a movie. This is fun stuff, there's no right or wrong, there are probably a few laughs along the way, and this is a good icebreaker to get at the more serious and personal decisions of who is going to fill out your marketing team. Whichever one you do, discuss the choices and rationale for the key picks.

## FAVORITE RESTAURANTS

Food is love and we all love food. What are some of your favorite restaurants and why? Is it the love of the food? The service? The ambience? The price points? To the restaurateur it's all part of the business. To you it's the stuff of enjoyment—customer satisfaction. What's the merger of the two that you can extend to your business?

# Acknowledgments

"Share the glory."

—DAVID CARRADINE

## PAUL KURNIT

Special thanks to everyone who inspired me on my journey called marketing, who showed me it was okay not to be a "creative guy" because marketing, at its best, is a rich, creative enterprise.

Big thanks to our publisher, Adrian Zackheim, who immediately recognized that Marketing Plan in a Day was the Big Idea for the book we needed to write. To our editor, Adrienne Schultz, whose comments sharpened the content in the editing. To Will Weisser and Laura Clark and their team at Portfolio for their support in getting the book out there in front of the people and in the places it needs to be.

To my wife, Susan, who is the most intuitive marketer ever, and to my kids, Ara and Jesse, who taught me what sells and what doesn't every day growing up.

To my father, Shep, who risked big and won big in bringing

powerful ideas to the marketplace, and to my mother, Jean, who to this day refers to grocery shopping as marketing.

To my brothers, Rick and Scott, who surround marketing in their legal and Internet careers and treat marketing as a full-contact sport.

To Steve's and my PS Insights team: Norm Siegel, world-class art director; Doug Olney and Jeremy Berger, who make sense of the world on film; Danielle Cacnio, Web designer extraordinaire; Rhonda Vanover, whose stills capture the soul; and Dan Lance and Mark LePatner, who turn video editing into delicious Web bites.

To Peter Hurley, whose head shots are way more than a head above and who has the wisdom to crop below the baldness.

To all my marketing and advertising mentors, partners, colleagues, and clients—way too numerous to mention—and especially the people I had the privilege to work alongside over the years from Benton & Bowles, Ogilvy & Mather, Griffin Bacal, Hasbro, Pace University, and the myriad other contacts and collaborators who inspire me every day.

But most of all, profound gratitude to my business and writing partner, Steve Lance. Steve's *Little Blue Book of Advertising* was the first step in this writing ladder. Our coauthored booklet, *Advertising 2.Oh! Own the Content and Control Your Brand Destiny,* showed me a writing style I not only loved but one I could emulate. Steve writes as he talks—clearly, elegantly, engagingly. He protects me from convoluted prose and a tendency toward triples. He reminds me not to let great be the enemy of good. His commitment to commonsense quality got this book off the computer and into galleys.

So huge thanks, Steve, for enabling this book and ensuring it would be done. On to the next idea, the next insight, the next talk, and the next book.

## STEVE LANCE

To everyone I already acknowledged in our last book, I still feel the same way. But there are a few special dedications I have to mention this time around.

Many thanks to our publisher, Adrian Zackheim, for saying, "It's time for your next book." Also to our editor, Adrienne Schultz, for giving us the guidance and perspective to keep the process on track and on schedule. And to Will Weisser, Laura Clark, and the whole team at Portfolio for keeping our books in front of the people who matter.

To my previous coauthor, Jeff Woll, who now enjoys golf on a daily basis and still reminds me to keep a perspective on things.

To Norman Siegel, who continues to keep me honest—and who no longer reminds me that I'm not the best writer he ever worked with. Even though I still think he's the best damned art director in the business.

To the guys at Tallboy Films—Doug Olney and Jeremy Berger— who brought a camera to the party and keep us thinking young.

To Danielle Cacnio and Rhonda Vanover, whose senses of humor are as great as their talents.

To Max Lance, who's fast becoming the best writer in the family.

To Dan Lance, who continues to bring his artist's eye and subtle perspective to everything he does.

But most of all, I have to say something special to and about Paul Kurnit. The first time I saw him lead a Marketing Plan in a Day, I knew it was the most powerful tool I'd ever seen in my years in marketing. When Adrian Zackheim asked us for book proposals, I didn't hesitate to say that Paul's concept should become *The Little*

*Blue Book of Marketing*. I'm pleased and honored to be part of this effort; and while Paul may say that this book was a labor of equals, I have no doubt that it was his vision and commitment to a rational process that brought the whole thing to life.

So thanks, Paul. And here's to what I expect will be a continuing process of writing, communicating, and bringing insights to life.

# About the Authors

For nearly ten years, **Paul Kurnit** has been conducting Marketing Plans in a Day for a wide range of companies and start-ups. Before becoming an independent marketing consultant, Paul's career included managing the global business for Hasbro as president of DDB advertising agency, Griffin Bacal. While at Griffin Bacal, Paul started relationships with new clients by conducting simple, collaborative, in-depth analyses of their businesses. It was that process that grew into the Marketing Plan in a Day.

Prior to Griffin Bacal, Paul learned his marketing craft at Benton & Bowles and Ogilvy & Mather working for several of the finest marketing organizations in the world: Procter and Gamble, American Express, Kraft/General Foods, and Hasbro. Paul adopted a very simple philosophy: Great marketing and advertising happens only when everyone involved is working off the same set of plans and goals. There are no brilliant, game-changing ideas without inspired strategic direction and a creative marketing plan to drive great results. In addition to stewarding a range of top brands, Paul has written and spoken extensively about marketing, strategy, and creative innovation at conferences, in print, and in TV and radio interviews.

Paul is also founder of KidShop and Kurnit Communications and a professor of marketing and advertising at Pace University. Throughout his career, Paul has been dedicated to growing businesses through powerful strategic initiatives that have been translated into inspired marketing communications programs.

**Steve Lance** has spent nearly thirty years in advertising and marketing on the creative side of ad agencies and television networks, including his positions as creative director at NBC, associate creative director at Backer and Spielvogel, and creative director of the entertainment division at Della Femina, Travisano and Partners. He's created or been associated with some of the most memorable campaigns in television, including The More You Know for NBC and Shark Week for Discovery Channel. He has won numerous creative awards for his campaigns, including Emmy, One Show, Aurora, Mark, and Lifetime Achievement awards. He has been a member of the board of directors of The Copy Club of New York, a guest lecturer on promotion and advertising at universities and clients and advertising clubs across America, and he's coauthor of *The Little Blue Book of Advertising* (Portfolio, 2006).

Over the years, we've seen the pointlessness of creating advertising for clients who don't know what they're trying to achieve. The greatest ads in the world won't do a thing for a company unless the organization knows exactly where they want to go and how they plan to get there.

As seasoned business, marketing, and creative guys, we're independent thinkers who've been on the inside and the outside of big and small businesses, and marketing, creative, and entertainment organizations. As impassioned observers, bloggers, and speakers about the crosscurrents of marketing practice with life experiences, we understand that nothing gets accomplished without a clear road map. And finally, as a couple of guys with attention deficit disorder (Steve is diagnosed, Paul refuses to find out), we're impatient with wasting time or not moving smartly forward in life or in business.

In 2007 we founded PS Insights with our partner, Norman Siegel (www.psinsights.com). And since then, we've been developing speeches, presentations, workshops, training programs, marketing, branded content, and creative solutions for companies that share our vision of team focus and planning to drive personal satisfaction and impressive business growth. PS Insights is committed to helping companies of all sizes uncover the insights they already have about their business but can't seem to be able to bring to market. PS Insights is about helping those companies bring those ideas to the surface.

We invite you to join the conversation at PSInsights.com or e-mail us:

Paul@psinsights.com

Steve@psinsights.com

You'll also find us on Facebook, Twitter, LinkedIn, and just about every social-networking community. And if there's some new technology out there that hasn't been developed as of this writing, we'll probably be there, too!

July 2009